TAKING DOWN
BACKPAGE

TAKING DOWN
BACKPAGE

FIGHTING THE WORLD'S LARGEST SEX TRAFFICKER

Maggy Krell

NEW YORK UNIVERSITY PRESS   *New York*

NEW YORK UNIVERSITY PRESS
New York
www.nyupress.org

References to Internet websites (URLs) were accurate at the time of writing.
Neither the author nor New York University Press is responsible for URLs
that may have expired or changed since the manuscript was prepared.

Library of Congress Cataloging-in-Publication Data
Names: Krell, Maggy, author.
Title: Taking down backpage : fighting the world's largest sex trafficker /
Maggy Krell.
Description: New York : New York University Press, [2021] |
Includes bibliographical references and index.
Identifiers: LCCN 2020016795 (print) | LCCN 2020016796 (ebook) |
ISBN 9781479803040 (cloth) | ISBN 9781479803026 (ebook) |
ISBN 9781479803064 (ebook)
Subjects: LCSH: Backpage.com (Firm)—Trials, litigation, etc. |
Trials (Prostitution)—United States. | Human trafficking—Law and legislation—
United States. | Internet—Law and legislation—United States—Criminal
provisions. | Krell, Maggy. | Public prosecutors—California—Biography.
Classification: LCC KF225.B35 K74 2021 (print) | LCC KF225.B35 (ebook) |
DDC 345.794/02534—dc23
LC record available at https://lccn.loc.gov/2020016795
LC ebook record available at https://lccn.loc.gov/2020016796

New York University Press books are printed on acid-free paper, and their
binding materials are chosen for strength and durability. We strive to use
environmentally responsible suppliers and materials to the greatest extent
possible in publishing our books.

Manufactured in the United States of America

10 9 8 7 6 5 4 3 2 1

Also available as an ebook

This book is dedicated to the brave human-trafficking

survivors who have escaped and shared their stories.

Without them, there would be

no case,

no book, and

no anti-human-trafficking movement.

THE FUNCTION OF FREEDOM IS TO FREE SOMEONE ELSE.

— TONI MORRISON

CONTENTS

AUTHOR'S NOTE

THIS book is seen through my lens as a former prosecutor. The case information herein is public record. I have added to it my personal experiences and opinions. My focus is on female survivors of sex trafficking, based on the specific investigations I discuss, but there are also male, transgender, and gender nonconforming victims of sex trafficking being exploited in the United States every day. Additionally, this book focuses solely on sex trafficking, but equally egregious human trafficking is also occurring in many other industries, from restaurants and nail salons to garment factories and farms. Like sex trafficking, what's commonly referred to as labor trafficking is an extreme form of exploitation in which a victim is forced to work with little or no pay and is not free to leave. It is not the nature of the "labor"—whether it is sex acts or farm work or washing dishes—but the exploitation, the working conditions, the fear, and the lack of freedom that define human trafficking, which is widely referred to as modern-day slavery. As evinced during our investigations, many of the survivors of child-sex-trafficking come from unstable home environments or have suffered from sexual abuse as a child. Such circumstances have impacted their self-esteem and made them more vulnerable to predators. Because of underreporting, it is difficult to accurately define the scope of child sex trafficking in the United States.[1] In 2019 alone, the National Center for Missing & Exploited Children received reports on more than 10,700 children.[2]

I also want to recognize the growing movement of those who believe commercial sex should be decriminalized or even legalized. Indeed, it's important to acknowledge that not all commercial sex work advertised on the internet or anywhere else involves trafficking and exploitation. Sex trafficking should not be conflated with voluntary sex work.

This book is not about consensual sex work. It is about rape.

Those who want to see prostitution decriminalized or legalized have criticized the shutdown and prosecution of Backpage, claiming that this has made commercial sex more dangerous. The statistics don't bear this out. As a prosecutor, I saw firsthand the numerous rapes, robberies, and murders that occurred through Backpage. There was no screening, no criminal records check, no security provided. It was merely a criminal marketplace where people were sold. There was no way of knowing who would be at the other end of a call or text. Backpage made sex trafficking easy and lucrative.

The survivors who were part of the Backpage case were forced into sex trafficking, most of them as children. Their names have been changed in this book to protect their privacy. They were sold in multiple cities and sometimes in multiple states. They suffered long-term consequences and scars that will never heal. Those who escaped sex trafficking continued to suffer physically and mentally, struggling to overcome fear, anxiety, and sometimes drug addiction. And some victims of sex trafficking do not survive.

To be clear, Backpage never made any aspect of their lives safer. Backpage increased their suffering exponentially, made it harder to escape, and made more money for their traffickers. After the shutdown of Backpage, instances of sex trafficking decreased.[3] While other websites have emerged or expanded, there is no longer a centralized site where the sale of children is normalized.

Those who choose to engage in commercial sex work are just as deserving of law enforcement protection as the countless victims who are trapped in it. Research shows there are numerous health risks associated with engaging in commercial sex, which correlates with violence and homicide rates higher than those for the general public. Sex workers should not be stigmatized, ignored, or deterred from seeking justice. But that is a different book. The focus of this book is sex-trafficking victims and at-risk children who have been sexually abused—and what we did to stop it.

1

THE MOTEL

TOOK my seat in court with a stack of color-coded files. Each one contained a police report, a rap sheet, and a complaint charging the defendant with violating some specific section of the California Penal Code. Green files were DUIs. Purple were "regular" misdemeanors like bar fights or shoplifting or the occasional illegal cockfight. Red were domestic violence. I was sorting through them, attempting to match the order of my stack with the order on the court's December 7, 2004, calendar sheet so that I would be ready when the judge came out and began calling the arraignment names. If he called a name and I was not ready with the file, he would become impatient and make a dramatic scene about having to wait for me. The court's calendar was loosely alphabetical, except that there were add-ons. Add-ons were extra names that had been added to the end of the calendar. Half the calendar turned out to be the extra names, so there I was, furiously sorting so that I would not be fumbling through folders when the judge came out of his chambers and took the bench.

I was the prosecutor. My job was to seek justice on behalf of the people of the state of California, county of San Joaquin, and also to organize the color-coded files. Each of my files contained a story—about a person who made a choice, or a series of choices, that resulted in harm to another person and a law being violated. My job was to ensure that the individual responsible for the crime was held accountable, to insist on fairness, and to empower the victim.

Every morning, typically wearing a crisp, ironed, white button-down shirt, a black skirt-and-jacket set, pearls, and heels, I kissed my boyfriend, Cary Huxsoll, good-bye and traveled about fifty miles through thick Central Valley fog from Sacramento to Stockton, San Joaquin County's seat. I was only twenty-five years old, but I was tasked with decisions that would impact people for the rest of their lives, and I was trying to look at least thirty while doing it.

Just as I finished arranging the files, the judge took the bench. As the metal door on the side of the courtroom was closing, I saw a cluster of defendants in orange jumpsuits hovering by the door and peering into the courtroom. The bailiff now had to call them into the courtroom one at a time, in calendar order. After the bailiff and the court clerk consulted, the judge announced that he would be calling the in-custody female defendants first. This of course threw my ordering system completely out of whack, as I shuffled through the enormous stack trying to filter out the female defendants. It wasn't as if I could just grab Mary and Janis and Susie. The files were labeled with last names only, like Clark and Smith and Barkley, so I had to actually open them to determine the gender of the defendant inside. As I frantically reordered, the public defender and other defense attorneys started showing up. The public defender was there to represent anyone who did not have a lawyer, could not afford a lawyer, and wanted a lawyer, which tended to be almost everyone. There were a couple of private attorneys with private clients, there to obtain discovery (a copy of everything in my file), get their clients out of custody, and make sure the next court date coincided with their schedule.

The private attorneys would approach me, and I would pull their client's file. In many cases, we would agree to release from custody pending the next court date. Sometimes, based on the crime charged or the defendant's criminal history, I would argue that the defendant should stay in custody. The defense attorney would argue that his or her client posed no risk if released, and the judge would decide whether to reduce bail, release the defendant, or impose any other conditions. The private attorneys usually had other courtrooms they needed to be in for other clients at the exact same time, so they would ask the clerk if their cases could be called first. This meant more shuffling of the file stack, but by 9:45 a.m., the court finally started calling the 8:30 a.m. in-custody calendar. San Joaquin County Superior Court was in session.

The judge would read the name, ask the defendant whether it was true and correct, and proceed to read the charge: driving under the influence of alcohol or drugs; stealing from Walmart; battery; vandalism; prostitution. He would then ask the prosecution for an offer—a plea deal in which a defendant could accept responsibility for a charge at an early date in the proceedings and receive a lighter sentence than the maximum. This meant the defendant would be giving up a series of constitutional rights—to remain silent, to be presumed innocent, to receive a jury trial, and to subpoena and question witnesses against him or her. But it also meant that the defendant could receive a favorable sentence and move on with his or her life without being dragged through the criminal justice system and risking a more serious and consequential outcome. Some defendants did not get offers, either because the crimes were too serious or because the crimes required further investigation and were not suitable for early resolution. And so the judge made his way through the female in-custody calendar reading charges, advising defendants of rights, continuing cases for further proceedings, and taking pleas.

There were more female defendants than normal because there had been a sting operation over the weekend, ensnaring many young women who were selling their bodies for commercial sex.

All the files read the same: all the defendants were women. And they were all young, many of them teenagers. Almost all were African American. They were all being arrested late at night. The police reports and booking information listed their clothing, their address, and their property. The clothing was universally skimpy, consisting of short skirts, tank tops, and heels, even though it was December. The police report also listed the weather, which was in the high thirties. The property was typically a purse with a little bit of makeup inside, a toothbrush, forty dollars or less, and occasionally a few condoms.

The home address was almost always "transient"—the address that gets listed on the intake sheet if someone did not have or would not give the police an address and had no ID. The defendants were either homeless or wouldn't say where they were staying. Most of them didn't have an emergency contact to list when being booked into jail.

In court, they just wanted to get out of custody. They would say their names and answer the court's questions almost robotically. They would plead guilty if it meant getting out of jail. They stared blankly into space and looked numb and lifeless. They didn't seem to care whether the court appointed an attorney, whether the court pronounced their names right, or whether they gave up their constitutional rights.

The police reports described scripted encounters in which an officer working in an undercover capacity approached one of these young women and asked her to perform some degrading sex act for a small amount of money that he negotiated. She would agree and initiate physical contact, and then he'd give a signal to officers waiting nearby and she'd be arrested. It was freezing cold in a dangerous stretch of downtown. Anything could happen to these young women who were offering commercial sex acts to whatever perverted stranger drove up on them. And they never seemed to even have money to show for it.

Some people say prostitution is a victimless crime, but there in the San Joaquin County courtroom, I saw the defendants for the victims they truly were—thrust into scary Stockton parking lots on a nightly basis, nowhere else to go, no one to even call. With no money and no address, were they merely having sex for money to survive? What led these young women to this brutal place? Where were their families? Who was making money off their misery? And was anyone standing up for them?

For the first time as a prosecutor, I did not want to prosecute. I was supposed to be prosecuting people who made choices to harm other people or chose to violate the law. What choices were these young women making? Was there a choice? In the women before me, in the stories in the files on my desk, I did not see that they had any choice.

I got through the morning calendar without getting yelled at by the judge, and I wheeled my stack of DUIs, thefts, and vandalism cases back to my office. But I couldn't get my mind off the prostitution defendants. I sat at my shabby plastic desk eating a peanut butter and jelly sandwich and reading through the police reports again. I was picking a jury for an elder-abuse trial at 2:00 p.m., but I was fully engrossed in this stack of purple files until then. I noticed one other matching detail: all the defendants were being arrested in the parking lot of the same seedy motel on a corner near downtown. I did some more research. It turned out that the motel received dozens of disturbance calls from neighbors and had been the site for many sting operations. The motel owner had to know what he was profiting from inside those rooms. Why was this business able to profit from sexual exploitation?

What if, I wondered, we could target that motel? It was ground zero for this ongoing crime—a crime that I saw as a manifestation of human suffering. For a small amount of money, grown men were buying homeless teenagers in the motel parking lot. Instead of providing refuge to the teenagers and calling the police, I suspected that the motel owner was probably taking a cut on every single transaction. The teenagers never reported being victims; but that did not mean they weren't, nor would it necessarily prevent me from making a case.

Before our system of constitutional democracy, people fended for themselves. It was not the job of the public or the government to get involved when a bandit stole a man's mule, much less when a man hit a woman in the comfort of his own home. These were private matters between private parties, and the party with more power would usually win. There was no public mechanism for protecting the vulnerable. The relatively modern concept of a public prosecutor means that the public will protect the victim of a crime. When a defendant violates a law, he or she has committed a crime not just against one victim but against all of us, against society, against the people. And I was the attorney representing the people. My job was to enforce the people's laws, protect the integrity of the system, and stand up for vulnerable victims, including those who do not stand up for themselves.

Sometimes this was more challenging than it seems. I had domestic violence cases in which the victim would not want the case to move forward—she would recant her statement to police, say she had previously lied, and beg us to dump the case. Or she would not show up to court at all.

But those were sometimes the most important cases to prosecute. We had pictures of a woman with a bloody lip or a black eye. We had a 911 call with her sobbing and hyperventilating into the phone, gasping, "He's going to kill me." We had the officer who got to the apartment to find a terrified woman, a crying baby, and broken dishes. And when the officer found the suspect a few blocks away, we had a web of lies about where he'd been.

Because the prosecutor's role is not just to protect the victim but also to protect the public, we are empowered to file cases without victim cooperation, if we believe we can prove the case with the evidence we have. Victims do not always self-identify as victims because of the way they have been manipulated and because they have internalized so much trauma.[1]

I suspected that the women pleading guilty to prostitution might actually be victims, regardless of whether they identified as such or ever felt able to report crimes committed against them.[2]

When I wasn't in trial on a variety of domestic violence, vandalism, and DUI cases, I was discovering everything I could about that motel and attempting to build a case. I learned that the owner often worked the front desk, and he and his employees regularly gave out condoms to hotel guests. They rented rooms for short periods of time—less than a night. They had ongoing calls and complaints from neighbors and many visits from the Stockton Police Department.

One of the women working around the motel eventually explained how it worked. She said the men she met who were interested in commercial sex would walk into the office, ask the owner for a room key, pay cash, and even be given a condom. The owner would tell them to have a good time.

The owner was not just complicit in making a living off the commercial sex trade but was actually promoting it. It kept him in business, and he did not care that a teenager might be getting raped in one of his dingy little rooms.

Based on surveillance, cooperation from witnesses, and other evidence we were able to collect, I wanted to charge the owner with conspiracy and aiding and abetting prostitution. To my knowledge, no one had ever used that theory before to prosecute a motel owner.[3]

My supervisor was excited about the case from the beginning. His name was Chuck Schultz. He was bright and charismatic, and he brought incredible energy with him to work each day. If you ever had a case you weren't sure about, you could count on telling him the facts and him being absolutely outraged about what the defendant had done. "You're telling me he purposely busted his neighbor's fence? Of course you should go to trial on that! What a horrific thing for a person to do!"

Chuck was predictably furious with the motel owner for aiding and abetting in commercial sex acts, and he thought we could use the case to send a strong message by shutting down the motel and holding the owner accountable.

In 2004, laws criminalizing human trafficking were still in their infancy. Conceptually, the crime was akin to involuntary servitude or slavery, but the statutory framework was not applicable to what was happening on the streets. In California, sex trafficking was not yet defined as a crime in the Penal Code. But prostitution was a crime, one of the oldest on the books. And the concept of aiding and abetting—that anyone who knowingly helps facilitate a crime can be held accountable for that crime—is a long-enshrined legal principle. There was also conspiracy—agreeing with another person (either the sex worker or the sex buyer) to commit a crime and committing one or more overt acts toward that crime—such as supplying a motel room. And there was also pimping, knowingly receiving earnings from prostitution in whole or in part; and pandering, soliciting on behalf of or providing a place for commercial sex. All of these statutes were designed to stop the economic expansion of the sex trade. This motel fit directly within what the law was designed to prevent.

We charged the motel owner and manager with conspiracy to commit prostitution and pimping. Our theory was that in several individual instances, the owner received funds and provided a room, knowing that it would be used for commercial sex acts. The owner knowingly and willfully contributed to those crimes and received financial benefit as a result. As a backup plan, I had researched nuisance-abatement laws and city code violations that could have also taken the motel out of business. But I didn't want this to be categorized as a "nuisance." It wasn't about the neighbors who were complaining. It was about the proliferation of the commercial sex trade and how young, vulnerable women of color were being exploited.

It was a novel approach and caught the judge off guard, but it actually worked out. The motel owner was represented by a private attorney. We agreed to several terms, the defendant pled guilty, and the motel was shut down. It was a good first little step, but I knew that there was much more that needed to be done. We needed a cosmic shift in how we treated young people ensnarled in the dangerous life of the commercial sex trade. We needed to build cases against those who were quietly selling people for sex acts. And we needed to create a support system for victims. The images of those girls from that motel in Stockton were etched into my brain and would drive me throughout my career.

More than a decade later, their suffering became the inspiration for the biggest case I ever prosecuted. By the time I became a supervising deputy attorney general at the California Department of Justice, the seedy motel, I realized, had metamorphosized into a website: Backpage.com. Backpage was more lucrative, more prolific, and more evasive than the motel had ever been—but my legal strategy was the same: follow the money and disrupt the system.

2

OPERATION WILTED FLOWER

N the criminal justice system, prosecutors exercise vast discretion. We decide whether to charge a defendant, what crime or crimes to charge, and what deal to offer. Whether I offered to postpone a defendant's case for six months on condition that he or she sober up, show proof of steady employment, and turn in community service hours in exchange for dismissal of the charges, or take the case to trial and ask for the maximum jail sentence, would greatly impact the defendant's life and have ripple effects on the defendant's family. Based on the circumstances, either could be the appropriate move. And it was up to me, the prosecutor, to decide.

I got schooled by savvy defense attorneys and scolded by scrupulous judges. I made mistakes and tried to learn from them. I saw the suffering of both defendants and victims and learned that justice doesn't keep score. There is really no such thing as a win or a loss. Each day, you go in, you do your very best work, you seek justice, and you pray to God that you can leave a lasting impact and make your community a little safer.

The cases I handled helped develop my judgment and decision-making and taught me the rules of the criminal justice system. I learned how to value a case, when to make concessions and pick battles, and the importance of every single word a prosecutor says. I learned the value of talking to the jury after trial, I learned the importance of respecting the court and opposing counsel even when you vehemently disagree, and I humbly learned the impact that a prosecutor can have on the lives of both victims and defendants.

After gaining valuable experience as a local prosecutor, in 2005, I became a deputy attorney general in the division of criminal law, serving on the trial team. I would be handling larger, more complex cases originating across the state. I was thrilled, especially when I learned that a legendary prosecutor was working in the corner office down the hall from me.

I'd first heard of Dave Druliner when I was interning at the California Department of Justice in San Diego one summer during law school. He was prosecuting a big murder trial at the courthouse across the street. All the interns from our office were clamoring to get into the courtroom to watch him at work. An army veteran, Dave had been chief of the homicide unit at the Sacramento County District Attorney's Office before being recruited as the chief of the Criminal Division at the Attorney General's Office. But he didn't like managing the office—he wanted to prosecute cases. After a few years, he stepped down as chief but stayed on as a senior prosecutor, poring over the state's most complex homicide cases.

Soon after I joined the Attorney General's Office, I worked up the courage to introduce myself. Dave was over six feet tall and well built, with slightly graying, shaggy brown hair. He typically dressed in rumpled dress pants, orthopedic shoes, and button-down Hawaiian shirts in a variety of floral patterns and colors. Clad in my usual black-suit-and-white-shirt combo, I told Dave the kind of work I'd done in Stockton and the kind I wanted to do. I offered to volunteer to help on any of his cases. We clicked immediately. Dave was easy to talk to, and we had a lot in common: 49ers football, drinking Bud Light despite the growing trendiness of Sacramento's craft beer scene, basketball and particularly the Sacramento Kings, surfing . . . and the will to prosecute the most depraved and dangerous criminals in California.

Dave became my mentor and got approval for me to work with him on virtually everything. We drove around the state for various cases, like one in Bakersfield, where gang bangers had held up a barbershop, robbed and carjacked a district attorney investigator, and later killed a teenager during a home invasion. We prosecuted another in Susanville, where a mass murderer would have been released had it not been for our intervention. Another, which became Dave's favorite cold case, involved a San Francisco police sergeant who was gunned down in the prime of his life by a radical terrorist group in 1971.

Dave was an extraordinary lawyer. He was brilliant, dogged, and thorough. He was respectful and open-minded, listening to everyone: cops, victims, witnesses, defense attorneys and their clients. He never lost his cool, and if he felt stress, he didn't show it. "If you fall down, get up before anyone sees you"—that was one of his mottoes. He was also relentlessly positive. If a judge excluded crucial evidence we had submitted, Dave would find a way to argue that the ruling was somehow good for us. "This cuts both ways," he would say.

Dave was also fun to be around. I never got bored in the long car rides because he would tell an endless string of entertaining war stories about his cases and funny stories about his daughter and grandkids. When Cary proposed and we planned a wedding in Rosarito, Mexico, I knew Dave had to be there. He charmed my whole family and inquired about the relatives he met for years later. Dave valued family: he was excited for Cary and me as we started ours, even giving us a rambunctious black Labrador named LuLu who chewed her way through everything we owned (couches, Christmas-tree ornaments, and high heels). With Cary and me both having busy jobs as lawyers, Dave always reminded me, no matter what was happening on our cases, to find balance and make time for family.

We would also talk through cases, constantly gaming out scenarios in court and putting together cross-examination traps for defense witnesses. I had to remind Dave that just because he said something that sounded good didn't mean I could say it or do it—he had this special Dave power! Once we were at breakfast together in Susanville, and he was slowly making his way through a bowl of oatmeal. I had finished my coffee because I don't eat breakfast and was eager to get to court. It was after 8:00, and the judge would be taking the bench at 8:30. We had not been in front of this judge before, and I was going to be arguing a pretrial motion. The last thing I wanted was to be late. But Dave was taking his time and then ordered bacon just as the waitress was bringing the check. "You like bacon. You'll have some right? You gotta eat something," he insisted. "But I don't want to be late to court. The judge will yell at me." "No he won't. He won't even take the bench until 9:00." So I ate the bacon, and we got to court about 8:45. The judge was already on the bench and berated us for being late! "Counsel, we started at 8:30. You are late." Dave casually responded that he thought the hearing was at 9:00 and that we had been enjoying a leisurely breakfast up the street. I wanted to hide under the table. Dave went on to discuss his relaxing morning, throwing in that this his cocounsel, who doesn't usually eat breakfast, liked the bacon. And the judge somehow seemed calmed by it! "It sounds like you all had a nice breakfast. I should eat breakfast out sometime. Anyway, recalling the case of *People v. Bowen*."

We later laughed about it in the car, but I was still a little mad at Dave. There was no way I could have gotten away with what he had pulled off and no reason to be late! I was still a young woman trying to prove myself in what was still very much a man's world. There wasn't room for me to make mistakes like that.

After several years prosecuting murder cases with Dave, I badly wanted to create a new team, with undivided attention to human trafficking, a growing and largely unaddressed epidemic. While a new law passed in 2006 defining the growing scourge of human trafficking and providing for both civil and criminal remedies,[1] law enforcement still lacked the training and resources to enforce it.[2] This was different from the pimping laws, which criminalized receiving earnings "from a prostitute."[3] The trafficking statute included the element of force, fear, or coercion and recognized the person being sexually exploited as a victim. The California statute was similar to the federal Trafficking Victims Protection Act (TVPA), which had been codified a few years before.[4] The law was inspired by a 1995 case in California. A Thai garment worker escaped from a sweatshop in El Monte, a commercial city in Los Angeles County, where she had been held as a slave. The ensuing investigation led to the bust of the garment factory and the freeing of seventy-two other survivors, who had been lured to the United States through false promises and forced to work as slaves at a small compound enclosed in barbwire. The evolving legal landscape gave us new tools to go after traffickers.

I never forgot the women from the motel in Stockton. And it wasn't just sex trafficking of girls. There were male victims, transgender victims, and people being trafficked in a variety of different industries, forced to work with no pay and no freedom. There was an outspoken group of survivor leaders pushing for greater awareness and support from law enforcement. It was an insidious crime, hidden in plain sight and impacting the most vulnerable of victims. Yet our office, like most offices, had not dedicated resources to stopping it.

In 2010, I had approached the chief of my division and proposed starting a new unit with Dave Druliner that would focus on organized crime. In my mind, this meant human trafficking, but I pitched it more broadly. Instead, thanks to the mortgage meltdown, I was tasked with spearheading a strike force to combat mortgage fraud while Dave continued to work on murder cases. My chief said it was a "leadership opportunity," which is what management always says when they're assigning you something terrible that you don't want to do. (I have since used the line myself.) For the next few years, I labored in the financial weeds, rooting out and prosecuting unscrupulous attorneys, lenders, and realtors. It wasn't the work I was hoping to do, but it ultimately gave me a set of tools and a unique way to go after sex traffickers.

Eventually, we expanded the mission of the Special Crimes Unit to include organized crime. I was one step closer to adding human trafficking into the mix. Kamala Harris was attorney general of California, and with her background as the district attorney of

San Francisco, she already understood the problem well. In 2006, she supported the first bill to make human trafficking a felony. As attorney general, she doubled down on her commitment to the fight, supporting legislation to provide restitution to victims of trafficking and to enhance the penalties for trafficking of minors. She spoke frequently, and passionately, about the grave damage trafficking does to victims and communities and commissioned a report detailing its prevalence throughout California.[5]

I had no resources and no team. But I had a powerful ally at the top.

I received another boost in 2012, when Special Agent Reye Diaz transferred into our unit. Reye had a reputation as one of the best agents in the Department of Justice, but he had his own way of doing things and sometimes clashed with management. We'd met a few years earlier, when he was part of a gambling enforcement team and needed help getting a fraud case against a casino filed. He was frustrated that the locals initially rejected the case and pleased with me for ensuring that the case was charged.

Now, Reye and I were reunited and were turning our attention to human trafficking. We were both envelope pushers, looking for new challenges and opportunities to be creative. I hoped that a major successful prosecution that garnered media attention would persuade Attorney General Harris and her staff that we could use the criminal justice system to pursue trafficking systemically, rather than piecemeal, through low-level prosecutions. The overwhelming focus of law enforcement was still street-level prostitution busts. I wanted to go after the pimps and traffickers, the people making money off the exploitation of vulnerable victims. But these types of cases would take months to develop and would require additional personnel, as opposed to the one-night stings currently being orchestrated by local law enforcement and targeting either sex workers or their customers.

We zeroed in on a group of residential brothels and massage parlors that were either hiding in suburban neighborhoods or masquerading as legitimate businesses. In reality, they were selling young, vulnerable girls and women—often from overseas—for commercial sex acts. Many of these women were lured into Asian trafficking rings and brought to the United States with the promise of career training and advancement. It was similar to the tactics the traffickers used in the garment factory case in El Monte nearly twenty years earlier. The victims were often fleeing poverty, trying to make money to support loved ones back home. Sometimes they were escaping violence and persecution. Other times, they were simply seeking a better life.

That's not what they found. When they arrived in this country, they were told they were now thousands of dollars in debt and had to work to pay off the cost of their travel. Rather than working as professional massage therapists at spas or hotels, they found themselves forced into sex slavery. Sometimes they were told they only needed to sell their bodies for a few months, and then they'd be free to leave.

It was a lie. In addition to their travel fees, they now had expenses charged to them for room and board and security. They didn't speak English, they had no friends or family, no support network whatsoever, and they were told they'd go to prison or be deported if they talked to the authorities. Often, they weren't even allowed to leave the brothels. They slept in the same beds on which they serviced their clients. They were kept drugged—usually on ketamine, the date-rape drug—because an unhappy girl was bad for business. After a week or so, they were rotated to other massage parlors or brothels up and down the West Coast and in some cases all the way across the country.

These women lived their entire lives inside a succession of dirty little rooms, having sex with strangers for money. Those strangers found the brothels and massage parlors through websites such as Backpage.com and RubMaps, as well as word of mouth, ads in foreign-language newspapers, and even business cards handed out at swap meets, casinos, and bars. We were able to track some of the advertisements. We learned that the men came from a variety of different backgrounds. Some were married and wore suits to work. Others worked at construction sites. Reye once followed a suspected brothel customer to his office and learned that he was a dentist. Law enforcement officers were caught visiting brothels as well. We learned that while some customers were polite and attempted to charm the women, others were cruel and even violent. Regardless of their diverse backgrounds, they shared a disregard for the women they were exploiting and kept the sex-trafficking industry enormously lucrative. We were determined to do our part to shut it down.

But how? I had no interest in prosecuting the women themselves or arresting them to coerce cooperation, even though that was what other departments were doing. These women were victims. But they would never say so. And definitely not in court. Traumatized, ashamed, terrified of their pimps and traffickers, they were rightly fearful that talking to law enforcement could cause harm to a relative back home or their own injury or death. Interviewing them would yield no material evidence, probably not even the women's real names. How could we prove what the suspects were doing without their victims saying a word?

Fortunately, Reye was an investigative genius. He was creative and a risk taker. My job was to ensure that his unorthodox techniques would hold up in court. At all hours of the day and night, we texted ideas back and forth, as well as the occasional complaint about office bureaucracy or our floundering football teams (his was the Vikings, mine the Niners).

Ultimately, we designed a solid investigation that could be prosecuted regardless of victims' cooperation. The resulting plan was called "Operation Wilted Flower," and it rested on two novel strategies.

First, we decided to focus on white-collar offenses committed by the fake massage parlors—tax evasion, money laundering, failure to pay unemployment tax. These felonies fit comfortably within the mandate of our fraud unit, and because they were financial crimes, they would not require testimony from trafficking victims.

We still needed a way to get through the door of the brothels and prove what was really happening inside. This led to the second prong of our plan.

"How about I put some of my informants to work for us?" Reye said one day. He had a wide network of people who either were working off a sentence or had inside criminal information and wanted to help law enforcement. He was confident he could train some of them to go into the brothels and gather evidence.

I was far, far less confident. "Tell me how that would work," I said. "What exactly would they do?" As the lawyer in the room, it was my job to think through everything that could go wrong. When you're using civilians to infiltrate a sex-trafficking ring, that's a tall order.

"I'm thinking we wire up an informant for voice and video, have him pose as a john or maybe even as competition looking to set up a brothel out of town, and send him in," Reye said. "We could even give him samples of condoms or cigarettes or those knock-off designer purses, like he's trying to sell stuff." (Reye had access to unlimited quantities of confiscated counterfeit goods and illegal tobacco from previously serving on an underground-economy task force.) "Then we send him in and see what info he can get. It's worth a try."

"How would we ensure that the informant doesn't cross the line?" I asked. "How do we send him in as a customer and ensure that he doesn't have sex with one of the victims? How do we get him out of there without exchanging money for sex and still obtain valuable information? Won't this be suspicious to the owners? And we are *definitely* not selling counterfeit condoms! What if they break? That's on us!"

These were a small sampling of my many, many objections to Reye's plan. But another attorney on our team, Peter Williams—who was whip smart and had worked with Reye and his informants on a different task force—vouched for Reye's informants and helped me game out the myriad of legal issues.

So Operation Wilted Flower began. While Reye waited in his parked car at night, texting me more ideas about the case (and more complaints about the Vikings' offensive line), he watched his informants go into massage-parlor brothels. I have to admit that these men were masterful at obtaining evidence. Reye collected hours of DVD footage showing brothel owners describing which girls were for sale, how long they'd been there, when new girls would arrive, how much they cost—all the details of how the businesses operated.

With that evidence, we built rock-solid cases against the business owners, obtained search warrants, and planned our bust. We prepared extensively. Ten law enforcement teams would execute search warrants simultaneously in different locations, all in the middle of the night. Each team would be accompanied by victim advocates, lawyers, and translators.

It was not an easy operation to game out. We had an idea of what awaited us inside the brothels because of the footage the informants gathered, but we also knew that the men running the brothels were armed and trained to look out for intruders. Brothels were frequently the targets of robberies, and the locations we were looking at also did their own surveillance with high-tech camera equipment showing video of every car that drove by. There were serious officer safety concerns, as officers would attempt to enter the guarded headquarters of a criminal enterprise. But Reye had a strong background in mapping out precisely this type of operation from his years in the Bureau of Narcotics Enforcement at the California Department of Justice.

I was focused on doing whatever we could to support the victims. We wanted victim advocates who could speak the same languages of our victims, but we weren't always sure what those would be. It wasn't easy to predict. Before an operation, we couldn't tell whether the victims would speak Cantonese or Mandarin or Korean or some other language. We had some ideas based on the intelligence from our informants and the advertising the brothels were doing, but we could not be sure. And even if we were, it's not as if we had a bevy of multilingual social workers at our disposal. We were basically asking community volunteers who worked for a local anti-human-trafficking nonprofit to come help us bust a brothel in the middle of the night.[6] In the end, we game-planned the best we could with the limited resources we had. It was far from perfect, but it was a start.

I will never forget the brothel I entered as part of one of the arrest teams. It looked like a normal house in an ordinary neighborhood. In truth, it was a torture chamber, a hell for untold numbers of women. I stood in a mundane living room and felt sick.

Meanwhile, a chaotic scene surrounded me. Officers were arresting and handcuffing the owner, the men who worked the front desk and managed the women, and even some of the buyers. Other officers collected financial data, ketamine, condoms, large quantities of cash, stacks of white sheets and towels, and ledgers showing how many men each girl serviced per night.

And two young, terrified women sat on the living-room couch, staring at the ground. We did our best to help the women we found in the brothels. They had been dehumanized in the most brutal of ways, and we wanted to give them dignity and a chance at a better life. But there was only so much we could do. As we had predicted, the girls and women from Operation Wilted Flower did not want to provide information or appear in court. They just wanted to return home to their families. Our criminal complaints against their pimps were vague about who these women were. Often, we had no clear idea of their ages. Fifteen? Sixteen? Twenty? We rarely knew their real names. They were described as "Jane Doe 1, identified as female wearing bikini, in a house of prostitution, located at 7200 Tamoshanter Way," "Jane Doe 2, identified as 'Yaya' in a house of prostitution," "Jane Doe 5, identified as 'Sherry or Shelley' in a house of prostitution," "Jane Doe 9, identified as 'a Chinese girl' in a house of prostitution," "Jane Doe 10, a Malaysian girl," and on and on.[7] The victims present during our takedown operations were not the same victims we saw during the informant infiltrations. The descriptors we used were taken directly from the images and conversations in the recordings. We tried to identify and locate the women in the recordings, but it was nearly impossible. Even though they may never know it, we would seek justice on their behalf.

By using our audio and video evidence, corroborated by items seized during the busts, we were able to charge the traffickers with conspiracy to commit pimping, tax evasion for not paying unemployment insurance taxes, and in one case even bribery of police officers (officers posing as corrupt officers collected as much as $2,000 per month to look the other way).[8] Even without victims' statements, we had abundant evidence that the owners were knowingly receiving commercial sex proceeds and could prove additional financial crimes.

Using the same strategy, we gathered intelligence and obtained convictions against multiple traffickers throughout California, working our way up into larger and larger trafficking rings. Ultimately, our operation became a roadmap for investigations throughout the country.

Many people believe there is nothing wrong with two consenting adults agreeing to sex acts for money.[9] There is a social movement growing around women who argue that they are freely choosing to be sex workers, and I would not judge them or discredit their feelings and choices. But throughout my career as a prosecutor, the women I came in contact with who were selling their bodies for sex acts were anything but free. Even those who purported to be willing sex workers had long histories of childhood trauma and sexual abuse. Many were selling their bodies out of sheer desperation and extreme poverty, as opposed to choosing from a plethora of career options. Statistically, the path to sex work often includes being raped or molested at a young age, being sexually exploited by a trafficker as a teenager, lacking a stable family environment, running away from an abusive home or group home, growing up in the system, and never experiencing consistent, unconditional love.[10]

While a commercial sex transaction may seem consensual on the surface, the lopsided power dynamic, the history of trauma and abuse, and the lack of options often make the consent illusory. And sex without consent is rape. The exchange of money doesn't change that.

The women involved in Operation Wilted Flower clearly were not choosing to be sex workers. It really can only be a "choice" if there are other choices to choose freely from; for these women, and for many others, there weren't.

With their distress in mind and a successful operation accomplished, we expanded our efforts to combat human trafficking at the Attorney General's Office. What we found as we dug deeper into this insidious industry is that, contrary to popular myth, the vast majority of sex-trafficking victims are born right here in the United States. No international borders are crossed. No language barriers exist. But manipulative promises are made, and the outcomes are devastating.

Now, we had a powerful way to stop it.

3

AMERICAN SEX TRAFFICKING

"You posted an ad online, correct? And that's how you met him? Why didn't you run away from him? Why didn't you call the police? You had a phone, correct? Did you call a friend? Why didn't you call anyone and ask them to pick you up? Why didn't you flag down the police? Why didn't you call your mom? Why didn't you just go home?"

Tasha was being asked these questions over and over again by a belligerent attorney named Matthew Fletcher. Fletcher was a notorious defense lawyer who had represented the rap mogul Suge Knight. He had a brash, unapologetic style. He frequently came to court late and unprepared. I often provided him with pens and copies of his own motions just so we could get started. He was also temperamental, losing his cool to the point that the court would have to take breaks and ask that he calm down.

His client, Andrew Jordan, was on trial for sex trafficking.[1] This was the preliminary hearing, where the judge would decide if there was enough evidence to move the case forward to a jury. Both Jordan and Fletcher were large men, standing over six feet tall, weighing well over two hundred pounds, with shining, clean-shaven heads. Jordan was cocky, seemingly invincible, and even though he was facing over twenty years behind bars if convicted, the hearing was a show for him. He sat there smugly, passing notes with Fletcher in seeming admiration of Fletcher's antics, while Tasha cowered on the witness stand, fielding a barrage of questions meant to intimidate, bully, and belittle her.

Like most human-trafficking victims, Tasha did not feel she had anywhere to go or anyone who could help her. She didn't have family she could turn to. Like most traffickers, Jordan was a seasoned manipulator and had convinced her, throughout their relationship, that anything she endured was her fault, that no one would ever believe her, and that he would kill her if she went just an inch in the wrong direction. He monitored her every move. He checked her cell phone. He counted the number of condoms he gave her each night and counted the amount of money she brought back. She lived in constant fear.

Thousands of girls like Tasha were being sold for sex acts every night, mostly on a website called Backpage.com.[2] In the United States, a disproportionate share of the victims are African American girls and women.[3] By 2014, Backpage operated in eight hundred cities across the world, and for a small fee, anyone could sell anything. The site looked similar to Craigslist, a regular website for classified advertisements, but the site was most commonly used for the sale of human beings. Traffickers could sell victims over and over again on a nightly basis, using the site's escort section and merely a cell phone. Even if a family member was driving around looking for their missing kid, they'd never find them on the street—they were often hidden in motel rooms in cities three states away, thanks to Backpage. Some moms and dads spent night after night looking, with no idea that their daughter was in trouble in a different time zone.

But many of the kids who are trafficked don't have parents out looking for them—they are "system kids" who have bounced around foster care, juvenile hall, and group homes without experiencing a support system, a stable home, and unconditional love. These kids are targeted by pimps and traffickers particularly because of vulnerability factors that make them more susceptible to manipulation.

Tasha had a strained relationship with her mom, who lived in Texas. She was supposed to be going to school in California but instead had met Jordan. Her dad and brother had died, and her most precious possessions were the urns that held their ashes. Tasha thought Jordan could fill the void they had left and provide her some stability. Instead, Jordan took her financial-aid check and coerced her into selling her body for sex.

As Tasha testified, Fletcher zeroed in on every mistake she made—every picture in which she stood with Jordan and smiled, the time she "agreed" to get his name tattooed on her wrist and chest, and all the times she "could have" run away. To prove human trafficking, the prosecution must show that the defendant deprived the victim of her personal liberty and used force, fear, or coercion to make her engage in commercial sex. How could we possibly prove that when she wasn't physically restrained or locked in a room? he argued.

But like so many victims, Tasha was anything but free. Jordan was tracking her every move. She wasn't allowed to return until she'd reached a nightly money quota, called a "trap." She had a specific geographic region she was allowed to work in, and if she went outside the boundaries, she'd be beaten. She did, and she was. After each sex act, she had to text Jordan a smiley face, indicating she had completed it and collected the money. Whether she was sick, tired, or bruised from the prior night's beating, she had to work.

Because Jordan said so.

He also held her father's and brother's urns hostage. They were the only possessions she cared about. He'd threaten to throw the ashes away when Tasha disobeyed him. One time, while hurling abuses at her, Jordan threw her dad's urn onto the cement, breaking it. After that, Tasha carried her father's ashes in a plastic bag.

Finally, when she was in custody for prostitution in the Los Angeles County jail, she confided to a deputy that she was scared to get out. That small, brave comment led to the investigation that led to Jordan's arrest, just as he was coming to jail to pick her up. Instead, Tasha was released, and Jordan was arrested.

I charged him with sex trafficking and worked the case with the Long Beach Police Department and Jessica Owen, an eager new attorney who worked out of our Los Angeles office in the Appeals, Writs, and Trials section. Jessica was inquisitive, enthusiastic, and persistent—this was her very first trial case, and she would leave no stone unturned. While I often found myself explaining why her ideas would not work, I was impressed with her questions and nonstop pushing. From Jordan's criminal history, we discovered that he'd been arrested (although never convicted) of domestic violence. Jessica insisted on tracking down the old file, correctly predicting that it would contain important information. The victim was Alicia, and if we could find her, she could possibly corroborate Tasha's testimony. Alicia had multiple convictions and arrests for prostitution during the time frame that she was with Jordan. This meant there was a likelihood that Jordan had trafficked her as well.

Since the statute of limitations for human trafficking was six years, if I could find Alicia, there was a possibility that if she was trafficked, we could add her as an additional victim. Before a felony case goes to trial, the prosecutor must first prove that she has enough evidence or "probable cause" to move forward. This usually occurs at a preliminary hearing in front of a judge, but it can also happen in front of a grand jury. Unfortunately, we had not been able to locate Alicia before the preliminary hearing. But on the eve of trial, we were able to find her, living with family in a suburb north of Los Angeles.

I met with her, her mom, and her dad in a conference room at a small police station near her hometown. She was in her early twenties but looked about sixteen years old with soft caramel brown skin and slight dimples. She was also pregnant with twins. I knew she would not want to talk about her ex-boyfriend, let alone sex or commercial sex, in front of her parents, so I asked them to wait outside. She was still very reluctant. She seemed to harbor mixed feelings about Jordan, vacillating between being terrified that he would find out if she talked to me and being concerned that if she told me what happened, he would go to prison. Even though years had passed and he had been extremely abusive, she still had feelings for him. Like most victims who have endured long-term trauma, she didn't tell a chronological story from beginning to end. She shared bits and pieces, and there were many parts of the story she did not remember or she did not say. At times she was incoherent, and other times she was holding back. But she told me enough to get the picture, and it was very familiar. I also could not help but notice tattoos on her wrist and neck, which said "Andrew" and "Jordan," respectively—perfectly matching the branding that had been placed of Tasha's wrist and neck.

I also met one-on-one with each of her parents. Her mom told me that there were hundreds of times that they got hysterical calls in the middle of the night, that they drove around the worst parts of LA looking for her, that they found her once with bruises all over and no shoes, that when they "visited her," they would meet at McDonald's and Jordan would sit in his truck and watch. Their visits with their daughter were monitored by Jordan like they were prison visits. Alicia's mom said she went to law enforcement, and they treated her terribly—they said since Alicia was over eighteen years old, there was nothing they could do. She wasn't a runaway. Once Alicia ran into a police station for help; but they considered the incident mutual combat, and no charges were filed. Alicia's mom said that it was because Jordan had connections in law enforcement. I doubted this was true or that it would make a difference. But because Alicia and her mom believed it, they would never feel protected by law enforcement.

Alicia's mom asked if I had kids. I had two at home. "What would you do if this happened?" she asked me. As much as I wanted to convince myself that this could never happen to me, in my little safe world with the emotional walls I had carefully built, having kids makes all of us vulnerable. While my heart was sinking and my mind was racing, my professional instincts kicked in. I said something neutral, professional, and reassuring, but inside, my heart broke for her, for everything she and her family had gone thorough. She was wrought with guilt, questioned every parenting move she made, everything she hadn't provided, and every red-flag behavior she hadn't noticed. Even though Jordan had been out of their lives for years by this point, the emotional damage persisted.

Alicia's dad echoed her mom and filled in additional details. He was in poor health and needed dialysis. You could tell that he had been aged by the stress of parenting Alicia, in addition to his own challenging life and failing health. He was ashamed by what had happened and blamed himself, saying things like, "I wasn't a perfect dad." And he wasn't. Still, he was a proud man and a protective father. He shared one episode when Alicia came home to visit and Jordan wouldn't stop calling. Alicia's dad finally picked up the phone and exchanged expletives with Jordan. Jordan threatened to kill him and rape his wife. "I could have fought with him. . . . You'd probably be prosecuting me right now." Alicia's dad was heartbroken over everything that happened but grateful that his daughter was finally through with Jordan and that justice was coming.

But in order to seek justice for Alicia, I would have to dismiss the case so that I could refile it with an additional victim and additional charges. There is a "two bites at the apple" rule in California, so you are allowed to dismiss a felony case once and then refile. It isn't considered "double jeopardy" because jeopardy hasn't attached yet—the defendant has not been convicted or acquitted, so the factual issues have yet to be fully determined. This happens sometimes if you are set for trial and can't find a witness and the court will not grant a continuance or if an additional defendant or additional crimes are identified and need to be charged. It is unusual, but sometimes the prosecution actually needs more time and the defense insists on a speedy trial, so dismissing and refiling is the only way to stop and restart the clock. This is rare, though. It is much more likely that the prosecution is insisting on swift justice and the defense is delaying and asking for more time.

Normally, if the prosecution does dismiss, the dismissal happens early on in a case while the case is still being evaluated and investigated, not on the eve of trial, after a preliminary hearing, when the case has been set for months and the defendant is waiting in custody for his "speedy trial." Matthew Fletcher and his client would be furious, and the judge would not be happy either.

If I didn't dismiss the case, I could still use Alicia as a witness to corroborate Tasha's testimony, but Jordan would not be convicted of any additional crimes on the basis of Alicia's testimony. Jordan had been in custody since his arrest. The case had been moving quickly because he had not waived time, meaning that under California law, he was guaranteed his preliminary hearing (where the judge finds probable cause) within ten days and then his trial within sixty days of arraignment on the information. The information is the charging document that is filed after there is a holding order on the preliminary hearing complaint. So there I was with a difficult choice to make.

On the one hand, dismissal was tricky. I would have to relocate both victims in a few months. I would have to get through a preliminary hearing again. Jordan could argue that the prosecution violated his due process rights with this last-minute change of plans and was abusing the court system. There was also the chance that the judge could let Jordan out of custody, not wanting to hold him since the case was being dismissed, even though it was being refiled. Even if I could arrest him on the new complaint, I didn't like the idea of him getting out of custody for any period of time. Jordan was both a flight risk and a danger to the community—if he got out, he could terrorize these victims, who were already so fearful of him. But I was bothered by what Alicia's mom said about law enforcement never believing them. Alicia's victimization seemed to continue long after she left Jordan because she still seemed to blame herself. Alicia's mom said the cops never saw her as a victim—just as a criminal. Indeed, she had the criminal history to prove it: arrests and convictions for prostitution throughout the period she was "dating" Jordan. And there was the time that she ran into a police station for help, and they decided it was "mutual combat." I knew that this background could go both ways with a jury, but I hoped to show the jury that she was a sex-trafficking victim trapped in an abusive relationship.

Ultimately, I decided that seeking justice on Alicia's behalf was worth the risks. Getting yelled at by a judge was nothing new for me, and I thought if I did it right, I could keep Jordan in custody. On the morning of trial assignment, I dismissed the case against Jordan in open court. I explained to the judge that an additional victim had been identified, and a new complaint was being filed right then and there by my colleague Jessica Owen in Department 2, where new cases are filed, and that if the court would be so kind as to transfer the matter to Department 2, Jordan could be arraigned on new charges without further ado.

Jordan and Fletcher were red-hot mad. But the court wasn't. The judge was happy to have one less trial to find a courtroom for, and the fact that he could immediately send all of us to Department 2 without having to listen to Fletcher's temper tantrum was a plus. So the judge ordered the bailiff to send Jordan to Department 2. Fletcher was still frothing at the mouth, but the judge cut him off, pointed to Department 2, and called the next case. I was scared to even cross Fletcher in the hallway. I went the long way and scurried down the stairs in the back of the building. He was still cussing as he walked into Department 2. He ranted at the judge and demanded that his client be released immediately. I responded that the defendant was being charged with two counts of human trafficking and that the victims were in fear for their lives. "The procedural backdrop shouldn't matter, your honor. The fact is, he is highly dangerous—his criminal record proves it—and he's made threats in this case." The judge kept him in jail and set the case for preliminary hearing.

Jordan filed a series of motions, all of which were denied. We made it through a bumpy preliminary hearing, using an officer's testimony rather than calling Alicia or Tasha as live witnesses. Eventually we made it back to trial. Tasha was prepped and had kept in touch with the victim coordinator fairly regularly. Alicia was a challenge. We were able to serve her with a subpoena, but I still thought there was a good chance she would not show. I knew that if she didn't show, I would have to dismiss the charges against her and proceed only with Tasha. But justice for Alicia was worth the risk. My plan was to call her mom as the very first witness. Then I would call her and then, briefly, her dad. But I needed her to come to court for any of this to work. Jessica was nervous: "What if she doesn't show up? What will you tell the court then? Or what if she doesn't testify consistent with her statement? What if Jordan somehow gets to her?" Maybe I would get burned. But I believed in Alicia and also believed that this moment could be terrifically empowering for her and her family.

Reluctantly, Alicia came to court. She seemed genuinely surprised that she had really been named as a victim in the case.

When Alicia first was sworn in as a witness, I wasn't sure she'd say anything at all. She was terrified. But sometimes silence is more powerful than any words. She looked down and said her name in a soft, shaking voice. The damage Jordan had done to her years ago was clearly still devastating.

Alicia showed the jury her tattoos, the same as Tasha's—it was Jordan's name branded on her wrist and chest. She slowly testified about the same control mechanisms, the rules, the money, the text messages.

Fletcher blasted her with questions and accusations. Every mistake she'd ever made was on trial. And despite a pretrial ruling from the judge that the defense was not to discuss her sexual history, Fletcher ran right through the ruling, making her out to be a career prostitute who got what she deserved.[4] I would object, the objection would be sustained, Fletcher would be reprimanded, and then he'd continue right where he left off. I knew that he was dead wrong and it was phenomenally unfair, but the more I reacted, the more it could look to the jury like the prosecution had something to hide. So I let them "bathe in the evidence," as Dave would say. And despite the mistakes Alicia had made and the life she had lived, she never wanted to sell her body for sex, and that's what Jordan made her do. The mistakes made her the perfect victim, I would argue. Predators like Jordan find girls who are vulnerable, girls like Alicia and Tasha.

We also called an expert witness to testify about the cycle of abuse and trauma that prevents many domestic violence victims, including human-trafficking victims, from leaving abusive relationships. I had asked a close friend from college, Kathy Ta, who was now a standout prosecutor at the LA District Attorney's Office for an expert witness she could recommend. She gave me a well-known, articulate, and experienced social worker who had worked with a Los Angeles County Domestic Violence Task Force and interviewed hundreds of abuse victims as well as abusers. Kathy's only warning was not to let the social worker draw her "control wheel" in court. "It looks like chicken scratch," Kathy said. "You'll lose the jury."

Without ever meeting Tasha or Alicia, the expert explained how victims become trapped in abusive relationships. She gave examples of verbal abuse, threats, embarrassment, and physical abuse that abusers use to keep their victims feeling powerless. She testified that domestic violence is a pattern of coercive control in which there is a series of tactics that are used within the relationship to convince the victim to think, feel, and behave as if the abuse they are experiencing is normal, it is their fault, and it is something that the victim, not the perpetrator, has done wrong.[5]

The expert's description perfectly fit the tactics used by Jordan. Alicia described him calling her ugly and cutting off her hair one night. It was punishment for her not bringing in enough money. When she cried, Jordan laughed at her and made her feel stupid. She felt as though if she told anyone, they wouldn't believe her or would think she was ridiculous. She was already a "prostitute," so no one would care about her, she believed. Alicia's testimony was both heart wrenching and believable. If anything, she still minimized Jordan's abuse but described him with such palpable fear that his utter dominance and control over her were clearly displayed.

Tasha's testimony also perfectly fit the pattern of abuse that the expert witness described. She was taken out of bounds once by a customer, off the two-mile grid that Jordan had designed. She was gone longer than normal. When she returned, Jordan took the money and beat her relentlessly. She was terrified. "You can't call the police," he said. "What, you think they'll believe a prostitute? You disrespected me. You broke the rules. This is on you."

There was an easel with a large notepad behind the witness stand. Before I could intervene, my expert witness smiled at the judge and said, "Your honor, may I use this to illustrate my point?" "Certainly, ma'am," he replied. *Here we go*, I thought. When she first drew the outline of the wheel, it looked okay, but as she filled it in, layer after layer, it became completely impossible to read. The jurors stared at it skeptically. I'd later argue to them that you don't need to be able to read this wheel to know what the defendant did in this case! I snapped a photo for Kathy, who got a kick out of it.

But the point the witness made was an important one, and it really sunk in with the jury. The wheel illustrated the tactics that abusive partners use to wield power and control over victims. This is the common core of all intimate-partner-violence cases, but in human trafficking, there is an additional layer of exploitation and sexual abuse and financial dependence. Central to my case was proving the deprivation of liberty, the lack of control that Alicia and Tasha had over their lives and their bodies.

Even though they weren't literally chained to a bed, I needed the jury to understand that they weren't free. Human trafficking requires proof that the defendant used force, fear, or coercion to obtain sex or labor. At different times, Jordan used each of these methods, the culmination of which forced the victims to engage in commercial sex on a nightly basis. While someone outside their situation might think there were ways to get away or that their actions appeared voluntary at times, both victims were being manipulated in a cycle of violence by an abusive pimp. Would the jury understand this?

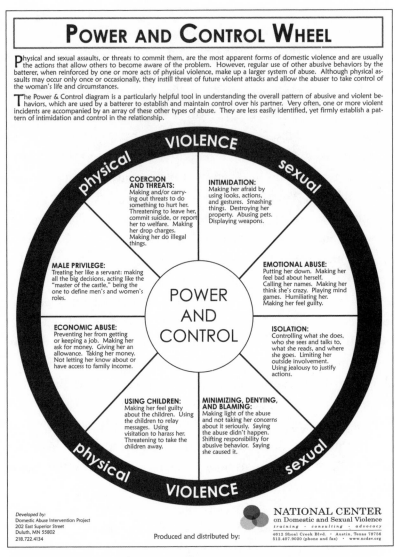

POWER AND CONTROL WHEEL

Physical and sexual assaults, or threats to commit them, are the most apparent forms of domestic violence and are usually the actions that allow others to become aware of the problem. However, regular use of other abusive behaviors by the batterer, when reinforced by one or more acts of physical violence, make up a larger system of abuse. Although physical assaults may occur only once or occasionally, they instill threat of future violent attacks and allow the abuser to take control of the woman's life and circumstances.

The Power & Control diagram is a particularly helpful tool in understanding the overall pattern of abusive and violent behaviors, which are used by a batterer to establish and maintain control over his partner. Very often, one or more violent incidents are accompanied by an array of these other types of abuse. They are less easily identified, yet firmly establish a pattern of intimidation and control in the relationship.

VIOLENCE
physical · sexual

COERCION AND THREATS: Making and/or carrying out threats to do something to hurt her. Threatening to leave her, commit suicide, or report her to welfare. Making her drop charges. Making her do illegal things.

INTIMIDATION: Making her afraid by using looks, actions, and gestures. Smashing things. Destroying her property. Abusing pets. Displaying weapons.

MALE PRIVILEGE: Treating her like a servant: making all the big decisions, acting like the "master of the castle," being the one to define men's and women's roles.

EMOTIONAL ABUSE: Putting her down. Making her feel bad about herself. Calling her names. Making her think she's crazy. Playing mind games. Humiliating her. Making her feel guilty.

ECONOMIC ABUSE: Preventing her from getting or keeping a job. Making her ask for money. Giving her an allowance. Taking her money. Not letting her know about or have access to family income.

ISOLATION: Controlling what she does, who she sees and talks to, what she reads, and where she goes. Limiting her outside involvement. Using jealousy to justify actions.

USING CHILDREN: Making her feel guilty about the children. Using the children to relay messages. Using visitation to harass her. Threatening to take the children away.

MINIMIZING, DENYING, AND BLAMING: Making light of the abuse and not taking her concerns about it seriously. Saying the abuse didn't happen. Shifting responsibility for abusive behavior. Saying she caused it.

POWER AND CONTROL

physical · sexual
VIOLENCE

Developed by:
Domestic Abuse Intervention Project
202 East Superior Street
Duluth, MN 55802
218.722.4134

Produced and distributed by:

NATIONAL CENTER
on Domestic and Sexual Violence
training · consulting · advocacy
4612 Shoal Creek Blvd. · Austin, Texas 78756
512.407.9020 (phone and fax) · www.ncdsv.org

Power and control wheel (Courtesy of the Domestic Abuse Intervention Project)

4

BACKPAGE

THERE seemed to be a never-ending pipeline of sex-trafficking victims, or sex workers, buyers, and street traffickers like Jordan. No matter how many traffickers were prosecuted, there would always be more. The long prison sentences hardly deterred anyone. And prostitution seemed to be an economic engine in impoverished neighborhoods. We were seeing sex, more and more, as a method of survival for poor women and kids. It wasn't really the sex that was the biggest problem, necessarily. It was the exploitation—the lopsided power dynamic we saw time and time again between the men buying sex and the people selling themselves, the vast number of people selling themselves who didn't keep their earnings, the number of teenagers and children, and the disturbing number of people who were being forced or tricked into a terrifying and violent cycle that they never chose and couldn't escape. I wanted a way to disrupt the entire system, to blow up the industry, to show the world what was happening, and most of all, to make it stop.

In Operation Wilted Flower, we disrupted a network of brothels in California. The smattering of defendants we prosecuted interrupted an otherwise seamless system of young foreign-born women being tricked into backrooms and sexually exploited. In the motel case in Stockton, we went after the neighborhood's biggest beneficiary of the illegal sex trade. Why should a business be able to knowingly profit and revolve its entire operation around illegal activity?

In the criminal justice system, the concept of aiding and abetting means that all suspects involved in a crime are held responsible, not just the person who burglarizes the house but the person who drives them there, the person who provides the crowbar to open the window, the person who surveils the house to make sure no one is home, and the person who helps exchange the stolen goods. It isn't just the burglar who enters the house but anyone who knowingly assisted in the burglary. Street traffickers like Jordan weren't selling victims all by themselves—they had the help of an expertly designed, user-friendly oppression tool, which recruited customers, kept victims on the market, and kept law enforcement at bay.

In 2013, the aider and abettor and the commercial sex industry's biggest beneficiary was a website: Backpage.com. Virtually every sex-trafficking case we prosecuted included an online ad posted on Backpage.com. The brothels from Operation Wilted Flower used it to advertise. The street traffickers like Andrew Jordan often sold victims to more than ten men a night using Backpage. Gangs used it to move victims around in a horrifying network of exploitation and violence. There was no doubt that Backpage exponentially expanded this growing criminal industry.

By 2012, human trafficking was recognized as the world's second-largest criminal business, with only manufacturing and sale of drugs ahead of it. It was crudely said that you could only sell a drug once, but you could sell a girl over and over again. Backpage made this much easier, more lucrative, and more exploitive to the victims. Backpage was operating in eight hundred cities throughout the world. At that time, every ad that was posted cost a small transaction fee, which could be increased for additional promotion. Like Craigslist and other classified sites, Backpage didn't appear to feature just sex ads. There were also sections for cars and jobs and furniture. The website was organized by country, state, and city and then by product. Within the "Erotic Services" and "Escort" sections of the site, there were pages of available men, transgender people, and other particularized options for sale. The largest section, and where our investigation focused, was of women.

Within the female section of the site, in any given city or town, there were dozens, if not hundreds, of erotic pictures. The pictures featured provocatively posed, almost-nude young women or girls, often bent over a bed, lying with legs up, or posed in a variety of sexual positions. The text of the ads included coded pricing terminology, such as "50 roses," and abbreviated sexual acts using initials and terminology utilized in the commercial sex trade.

Some of the people in the pictures clearly looked young. We saw girls we later determined to be as young as twelve advertised on Backpage during our investigation. Sometimes it was less obvious whether the girl in the picture was sixteen or twenty years old. There were other red flags we would look for, such as tracking phone numbers to determine whether a common line was being used to advertise multiple people. It was standard to see an area code nowhere near the city where the person was being advertised. The background in photos was often hotel rooms, which we tried to trace along with phone numbers to investigate cases.

Sometimes law enforcement would identify a victim and help her escape, then arrest and prosecute the trafficker, only to see Backpage recirculate her photo in a new ad. Whether the person in the photograph was the person who would be at the other end of the advertisement was also unknown. People could use and recycle old pictures for their own posts. It was unclear before the investigation whether Backpage was generating new ads using old ads. Regardless, this perpetuated the cycle of victimization for girls who were desperately trying to heal and move on from their trauma, only to have a Backpage ad recirculated.

I also kept this in the back of my mind as a possible legal theory—did Backpage really have permission to use these photos again and again? If the picture was posted without the victim's consent, and law enforcement notified Backpage that the person in the picture was a child-sex-trafficking victim, how could Backpage legally continue to use the image?

There was no doubt that the case was emotionally compelling. But shutting down an online crime scene was complicated by the Communications Decency Act (CDA), which protected online platforms in the spirit of extending the First Amendment to the internet. In addition to First Amendment arguments, Backpage would claim to be an internet service provider, rather than a creator of actual content. Its publishing and republishing of ads that others created, it would say, was protected by the CDA. Passed by Congress in 1996, the CDA protects internet service providers from liability for the words or actions of their users. Section 47 U.S.C. 230 says, "No provider or user of an interactive computer service shall be treated as the publisher or speaker of any information provided by another information content provider." Could Backpage be held responsible for the commercial sexual exploitation of hundreds of victims without having "created" the ads itself? Did Backpage contribute enough to the creation of the ads to be considered a content creator and therefore not protected as a mere platform for information from others? Could we argue that accepting commercial sex proceeds, a criminal act, was outside the immunity granted by the CDA? While Backpage and other websites had successfully defended against civil lawsuits using the CDA as a shield, there weren't cases involving state criminal prosecutions. Would a criminal investigation reveal that Backpage's business activity constituted criminal conduct and not protected speech under the First Amendment?

The CDA also specifically exempted "federal criminal law" from immunity and added, "Nothing in this section shall be construed to prevent any State from enforcing any State law that is consistent with this section. No cause of action may be brought and no liability may be imposed under any State or local law that is inconsistent with this section" (47 U.S.C. 230(e)(3)). As long as I could find a state criminal statute that was consistent with federal law, was there a narrow opening to prosecute a state criminal case against Backpage?

Carissa Phelps is a powerhouse advocate, public speaker, author, and sex-trafficking survivor. She was one of the most respected experts on human trafficking and was pushing for a change in law enforcement mentality—and rightfully so. Law enforcement's approach to sex trafficking was often misguided and unacceptable. Girls and women who were being exploited were too often being jailed for prostitution, and those who were forcing victims into virtual slavery were flying under the radar. It wasn't that officers didn't want to help victims; it's that they weren't always given the training, tools, and resources to identify or support victims. Victims rarely self-identified. It's not as if they say they are sex-trafficking victims and then officers arrest them. Instead, the victims tend to lie to protect their traffickers—they are trained to do so and are typically much more afraid of their traffickers than they are of going to jail for a few days. But with trauma-informed interviews, assistance from victim advocates, and the ability to provide supportive services to victims, much better, more just outcomes are possible. And this was precisely what Carissa had dedicated her career to.

It caught me off guard when Carissa wanted to meet and especially when she offered to come to the Attorney General's Office. Survivors and advocates were often reluctant to meet with law enforcement and were especially wary of coming to a law enforcement office. I was big on meeting folks in a place they felt comfortable and would speak freely. I didn't mind setting up meetings at coffee shops, churches, or nonprofit offices. I had done interviews in McDonald's and even one at a soup kitchen. But Carissa had a message to deliver, and she didn't care what room we were in. So there we were in the small conference room on the ninth floor of the Attorney General's Office.

"Every single victim I work with has been sold on Backpage. How much money do you think they are making on the backs of these victims?" she asked. *Good question*, I thought. *I need probable cause and a search warrant to tell you.* Carissa went on: "They think it is normal. Victims are not self-identifying because being sold online has been completely normalized, simplified, and commodified on that site. How do I convince a seventeen-year-old that it is illegal when it is so easy and everyone is doing it?" She pressed on: "You need to arrest the CEO and shut Backpage down. He is a sex trafficker. Hundreds of lives are being ruined by his relentless greed." She was right on. But I thought I'd flag the CDA in an attempt to explain why he wasn't behind bars yet. "It will be a real challenge," I said, "because of the CDA, but we are trying to build a case." "If you really think the CDA protects sex traffickers like Backpage, you ought to be doing everything in your power to change the CDA." She was right, again. "You started the first-ever human-trafficking team at the [California Department of Justice]. You've brought survivor leaders, nonprofits, and law enforcement together for the first time. You insist on trauma-informed practices and work up cases that go after major traffickers. And you know that the biggest trafficker in the industry is Backpage. You can do this."

I promised her I would do everything I could to build the case. She said, "If I help you with this, I want to know that you are going to stay on the case. You're not going into private practice or becoming a judge, right? I trust you with this." I had no plans to leave. She would be vouching for me with victims throughout the state, whom she had access to because of her unique background. If I was going to make the case, I would need to know those victims too. We were in it together.

After the meeting, I put a yellow sticky note on my sliding keyboard shelf with three aspirational goals: Get a felony conviction. Shut down the website. Fix the CDA (if it did in fact contain immunity for those who knowingly facilitated sex trafficking—an interpretation I wasn't convinced of just yet).

Before I could do any of those things, I needed an investigation plan. Long before arresting or charging suspects, you collect evidence and build a case piece by piece. Typically, evidence can consist of witnesses' or victims' statements, officers' observations, statements made by suspects, bank records of victims and suspects, email and other communications, or anything else that connects a suspect with a crime. To build our case, we wanted to develop probable cause to secure a search warrant for emails between Backpage executives. The emails would show who was running the company and how. It would show us how involved the owners of the site were in day-to-day operations and perhaps give us clues into how the money flowed into the company. Was Backpage really just targeted at commercial sex? Did those other sections advertising cars and furniture actually do anything? Where did all the ads come from? How did the company profit? And who profited? Did the owners really know what was going on? How cooperative were they with law enforcement agencies that were investigating sex-trafficking cases that used their site? What was the scope of the business, and how much of it was illegal?

To gain access to company emails, a judge must sign off on a search warrant that articulates probable cause that evidence of a felony will be found at the location. If a person was suspected of dealing drugs, for example, perhaps the search warrant would be for the drug dealer's house. The probable cause might be that officers watched a suspect collect cash from another party and then observed that suspect quickly run into the house and then run back out and connect with that same third party, handing him something. Based on these facts, the officer might set up a camera to monitor the house and observe frequent foot traffic in and out. The officer might then use a confidential informant to go into the house and perform a controlled buy, where marked cash is given to the suspect in exchange for narcotics. The informant would then tell the officer that he observed the suspect walk to a back room of the house and return with the narcotics. On the basis of all these facts, the officer has probable cause to execute a search warrant for that house. The officer would expect to find narcotics, scales, the marked cash and other money, and other paraphernalia indicative of narcotic sales. The evidence at the house also may be helpful in identifying the suspect and determining whether there are multiple suspects. The officer would describe all of these observations along with the address of the house he or she is seeking to search. A judge will then sign off, authorizing the officer to conduct the search.

But the case could also go in a different direction. What if the officers observed the suspect but were not able to get an informant into the house because of tight security? Instead, the officers observe the suspect driving to the bank. The officers determine the suspect's identity on the basis of his vehicle registration and driver's license photo. The officers continue to observe the suspect. The suspect frequently enters restaurants and clubs and doesn't appear to ever go to work. He regularly makes deposits at the bank. He doesn't have any registered business license, doesn't claim income, and appears to be unemployed. Now, on the basis of probable cause that the suspect is making frequent cash deposits, the officers do a search warrant for bank records. Rather than going to the suspect's house, which will immediately end the investigation by alerting the suspect that his house is being raided, the officers continue to work the case up by obtaining bank records. The records will show not only that he is making large cash deposits but also that he is wiring large sums to another account. Tracing this account will lead to another suspect, and so on.

In the Backpage investigation, we knew we were far from ready to storm the castle. We wanted to develop probable cause to obtain email addresses from whatever third-party server Backpage was using, if it was using a third party. So the first task was to determine how Backpage's email system worked, who housed it, and establish probable cause that evidence of crimes would be contained within those emails.

I met with Yiota Souras from the National Center for Missing & Exploited Children (NCMEC). Yiota was the general counsel for NCMEC and a tireless advocate for exploited kids. She knew all about Backpage, and she was excited that a law enforcement agency was committed to taking it on. She offered to help however she could.

It turned out that NCMEC contacted Backpage as early as 2011 because many of the children it had data on were being sold for sex on Backpage. Essentially, a child would go missing, and then her picture would surface in a Backpage ad. Backpage initially met with NCMEC and expressed interest in helping to prevent sex trafficking. But when NCMEC suggested steps that would impact Backpage's bottom line, it refused. For example, Backpage touted its monitoring system, which it claimed kept children off the site, but it refused to turn over rejected ads to NCMEC or law enforcement. This meant that in most cases, the trafficker could simply reconfigure the ad until Backpage accepted it. Rather than prevent sex trafficking, Backpage merely helped pimps thwart law enforcement. Within a couple of weeks of my written request, Yiota sent email exchanges, meeting notes, and internal notes that NCMEC kept documenting conversations with the Backpage owners.

I was finally getting a glimpse into who these guys were: James Larkin and Mike Lacey owned the company and would show up at meetings with NCMEC, along with shareholder/lawyer Don Moon.

Previous to running the world's largest online brothel, Lacey and Larkin had legitimately built a news-media empire, New Times Media. They had scrutinized politicians and spoken truth to power, but now they were sitting in a room, insulting the intelligence of NCMEC's professionals, and defending their right to run the world's largest online brothel. They were unmoved by the fact that children were being sold for sex on their website. Apparently, Lacey was so crude and inappropriate that the company sent a different representative to the next meeting. But the result did not change. Backpage was determined to continue to expand its sex-trafficking empire—the owners wanted to improve their image, but they never wanted to stop selling children for sex.

The information from NCMEC was key in that it showed us that the owners had been warned—they could not claim they did not know that children were being sex trafficked on their site. And worse, when given ways to assist NCMEC and law enforcement and prevent trafficking, they stopped showing up and continued to expand their business. This was helpful but not close to enough evidence to seize emails. We would not get a felony conviction by just showing that they were complacent; we needed to show that they actively participated. We needed more evidence.

NCMEC also regularly sent us lists of missing children advertised on Backpage in California. Sadly, we learned that California was one of the most dangerous states for at-risk kids. We were trying to interview these children without interfering with other cases, but it was sometimes complicated. Occasionally we got into tricky territory because street traffickers like Jordan would be prosecuted for selling a victim online, and a local prosecutor would be attempting to work with the victim to prosecute that case. We were trying to prosecute Backpage, essentially another trafficker but one organizational level above the street trafficker, and this could potentially create complications for the local prosecution. If the street trafficker was already convicted or not being prosecuted, we could meet with the victim without creating any issues for other law enforcement teams. But sometimes it was difficult to determine what the status of a case was or who the victims were.

Keeping track of all the moving parts was a challenge. But each piece of an investigation is like a building block. You gather block after block, and eventually you have enough to build something—in this instance, a solid legal case against the biggest sex trafficker in history. We tried to stay focused on our goal and not step on too many toes during the process.

From the information posted on the Backpage website, a nonprofit organization called Thorn began tracking data embedded in the publicly viewable advertisements and using analytics software to analyze it.[1] Thorn was founded by the actor/producer Ashton Kutcher, a dedicated partner in the fight against human trafficking and particularly child sexual abuse on the internet. If the traffickers used technology to exploit their victims, that technology should also be used to catch traffickers and protect children. Thorn's executive director, Julie Cordua, was eager to partner with law enforcement to protect children from sexual abuse. At the time, she was leading efforts to create an analytics program to identify children trafficked on the internet, using data from Backpage ads. On the basis of several analytical factors, Thorn designed a program to identify ads most likely to be featuring children. The idea was to save law enforcement the time of combing through hundreds of ads by focusing on certain ads that the software program was designed to flag. The program focused on keywords, numbers, pictures, and other data detected from the ads and known to be associated with younger victims.

We rented a motel room in Placer County with help from the local sheriff's office. Placer was just one county over from Sacramento and shared the same Backpage page. We couldn't get help from Sacramento because officials there didn't have the resources, but the Placer County Sheriff's Department was willing to help us run our operation. This was key, because I did not have the personnel to handle this internally. I was still struggling to get agents assigned to the investigation, which I had yet to convince the office was a priority, even though it was all I could think about. But with support from Placer, we organized an operation plan to identify and recover commercially sexually exploited children.

Thorn provided us a list of ads that its analytics program had flagged on the Sacramento area's Backpage site. An undercover officer would call or text the number on the ad and suggest a meeting place at the hotel. On some of the calls, the officer actually discussed the exchange of sexual acts for money. When the person on the other end of the ad arrived at the hotel, the undercover officer would lead her to a room and continue discussions involving the exchange of sexual acts for money. In every attempted transaction, there was enough to establish the baseline charge of prostitution. The purpose of a Backpage ad was unequivocally for commercial sex acts.

With the help of a local nonprofit organization, we steered the women we met to local service providers for assistance with various needs. Two of the women reported being homeless and were hoping to obtain a hotel room. Others were addicted to narcotics. At least one person eventually described being forced by a trafficker, whom we had already identified and followed after he dropped her off at the motel. We were able to successfully refer cases for prosecution where appropriate and offer assistance to victims we met during the operations.

One of the victims, Kim, agreed to cooperate with us against Backpage. She gave us a detailed explanation of how she utilized the site, initially directed by a street trafficker. Her story was heartbreaking yet familiar. She started going to parties as a young teenager. She got drunk and smoked weed and felt free. She stopped coming home and didn't think her mom really cared. She didn't have a stable home life, and when she met a guy who said he could take care of her, she was his. Soon after, he convinced her that they needed money and she was the one to make it. She was only fourteen the first time he posted pictures of her on Backpage. By the time we met her, she was eighteen and swore she was doing it on her own. She needed the money, and it was the only way she knew how.

Kim also told us about her little sister, Lizzie. She was sixteen years old and in juvenile hall, waiting to be sent to a juvenile facility out of state. She had been sold on Backpage many times as well, and we were able to find her ads up and down the state. Kim was emotional when talking about her little sister, who had been robbed of her childhood. In truth, both girls had been.

Overall, the result of the operation was devastating but not surprising—dozens of vulnerable teenagers and young women were being exploited for commercial sex, and Backpage was making a profit off every transaction. But this still was not quite enough to show probable cause to search the emails of Backpage's CEO. It was an important building block, but we needed more.

We still needed to determine who was running the company on a day-to-day basis, not just on paper. We needed his or her email address, evidence that he or she communicated by email, and finally, where that email server was stored. We needed to connect that person and his or her communications to a specific crime that was ostensibly being planned and carried out via email communications.

The warrant would need to be specific, not just a rant about a bad company doing bad things but an evidence-based justification, laced with specific, articulable facts explaining how the CEO was committing felony violations of California law and why evidence of the felonies would be in the emails. And if our charge was going to be "pimping," we needed to be able to eventually prove that the suspects were receiving the earnings of commercial sex.

5

THE BUSINESS

WITH the success of our first Thorn operation, we did another operation but in reverse. Using a credit card, which we'd later trace to Backpage's bank account, we posted a picture of an undercover law enforcement agent, included her phone number, and put the ad on Backpage.

It was quite an ordeal to get a picture to use. We couldn't use a picture from the internet, because we would be contributing to that person's exploitation or possibly violating copyright law. We also needed something that looked realistic, young, and sexy enough that people would call. No one wanted to volunteer to put their picture up, myself included! But eventually, an undercover officer from another department gave us her picture to use, and we paired it with an undercover cell phone.

The phone began ringing almost instantly and continued to ring for 806 slimy calls and texts within its first two days. At the same time, we advertised a couch for sale on Backpage.

The communications from the men who saw the escort ad confirmed without a doubt that they expected to have all of their sexual desires fulfilled by our undercover officer. Texts, voicemails, and conversations included negotiating "bareback" (without a condom) rates, insistence that oral and anal sex be included, demands for nude photographs and porn clips, and questions about "doubles."[1] I shuddered, knowing that many of the victims I knew through Backpage were being forced to advertise and were in fact children.

In addition to determining the demand for commercial sex services on Backpage, we also wanted to see whether the other parts of the site were being utilized. Were people actually buying furniture on Backpage as they did on Craigslist? Or was the entire site about commercial sex, and the other pages were merely a cover? The couch post answered that question, by receiving no response. It was a nice, well-priced couch that no one on Backpage was looking for.

By this point, Special Agent Brian Fichtner had been assigned to the case. Reye was busy with everything else and agreed to help out occasionally, but I could not get him assigned full-time. It landed in Brian's lap in a typical, shit-rolls-downhill-at-DOJ kind of way. He had just been assigned to the newly formed eCrime Unit, but his background was as a narcotics officer. He had never wanted to investigate "computer crimes" in the same way I did not want to take on mortgage fraud. Still, he had started his career as a juvenile probation officer and had the right demeanor for the case. He knew how to talk to teenagers. He was patient, unassuming, and kind. He was smarter than he let on and was a hard worker. I felt like if I could get him really hooked on the case, he was the right person for the job, even though I was sure that at first he wanted nothing to do with it. Early on during the investigation, he went out on medical leave for surgery on a torn bicep muscle, an injury he received teaching a tactical training course to other law enforcement officers at the academy. I was certain that his arm was fine and that he was just trying to get out of the case, hoping that while he was out on leave, some other poor mope would get assigned and then become so immersed in the case that there would be no role for Brian when he got back. But to my delight, Brian got bored during his four-month stint on the couch nursing his bicep injury and began digging into Backpage. He started texting me ideas for the investigation and contact information for some of the victims we had been trying to locate. When he finally came back to the office, he was all in.

With Brian's help, we continued investigating Backpage's business structure. Who were the company officers? Where did they live? Where were the offices? Who worked for them, and what did they do? Could we convince former employees to cooperate without alerting Backpage that an investigation was under way?

We knew that the company had been founded by James Larkin and Michael Lacey, the men who initially met with NCMEC back in 2011. Lacey was born in New York, went to Catholic school in Newark, New Jersey, and then attended college at Arizona State University. He protested Vietnam, vocally criticized his school administration, and generally clashed with authority. He ended up dropping out of college and started an alternative weekly newspaper, the *Phoenix New Times*, for the "sex, drugs, and rock 'n' roll generation."[2] He was never one to back down from a fight and had the words "HOLD FAST" tattooed across his knuckles. Larkin was an Arizona native with a kindred rebel spirit. The two immediately clicked, Larkin becoming the publisher and Lacey the chief editor of *New Times* as they began building a lucrative media empire. They used their newspaper to criticize politicians and continued to clash with authority, while reaching a broader and more expansive audience. In 2007, to make a point about their First Amendment rights, they published a grand jury subpoena that had been issued to their company, New Times Media. The sheriff then arrested them on flimsy charges. They were in custody for less than a day. And as soon as the charges against them were dropped, they were already filing a blistering lawsuit against the sheriff, which resulted in the county having to pay them nearly $4 million.[3]

We knew if we arrested them, we'd be in for a fight. In fact, we assumed that if they learned that we were investigating them, they would sue us and attempt to get an injunction stopping the investigation before it ever got off the ground. We had heard a rumor that this had happened to another law enforcement agency that had unsuccessfully attempted to investigate them. Even though I knew that it was a righteous case and that a lawsuit against us for pursuing it should fail, the distraction of the state having to defend itself while also trying to build a case could be crippling. If we filed charges while being sued, it could also look retaliatory. It was the kind of situation that could cause a pragmatic and politically savvy attorney general to drop the case and move on rather than to continue to dump resources into what could come off as a controversial First Amendment battle. But I never thought of it as a First Amendment battle. It was a sex-trafficking case.

As the paper business started drying up and online advertising became the future, Larkin and Lacey were in search of a more lucrative business plan. Carl Ferrer was a younger, techy guy from Texas with a background in internet sales. Larkin and Lacey enlisted his help to build Backpage and make them a lot of money. The news part of their business quickly went out the window, and they sold their news company shares to focus solely on expanding (and defending) Backpage.[4]

It turned out that Backpage's most lucrative product was teenagers. Rich, greedy, and no longer in the business of news, with Ferrer's help, Larkin and Lacey committed to cornering the sex-trafficking market, no matter how many lives were ruined along the way. On the outside, they looked like successful businessmen. They drove fancy cars, owned multiple homes, and traveled the world for meetings. Even as the news stories about sex trafficking on the site piled up, the business continued to expand.

A few days after our undercover law enforcement agent put up her ad for commercial sex, we wanted to test how quickly Backpage would take it down, if prompted by a law enforcement request. We also wanted to determine what role, if any, Carl Ferrer had in daily operations. We knew that Larkin and Lacey were the majority owners. We knew that Ferrer was the CEO, at least on paper. We didn't know whether any of them were physically in the office or how involved they were in running the site. We needed to show they had knowledge of what was taking place on their website on a daily basis. Later we would need to prove that they helped develop that content and purposely designed Backpage to function as a brothel. If we arrested them without establishing that knowledge, they could say, "We set this up as an advertising website, and we hired people who look at the advertising. If people are selling other people for sex on there, we had no idea and no involvement." Or relying on the CDA, they would claim that they were just a platform—a blank page where users could write and post what they wanted—and under the CDA's immunity provision, we could not prosecute them, as a mere platform for information from others.

That was exactly what we couldn't afford to let happen—we needed to build a case that would not only prove our charges but also deflate their defenses.

Normally, a law enforcement agent would send an email to a generic Backpage email address to get a sex ad taken down or request additional information about the poster. But Brian called Ferrer directly on his cell phone to see what would happen. Ferrer picked up. Referring to the ad number of the undercover officer, Brian explained that he was investigating a sex-trafficking case. "I suspect this is an ad for commercial sex," Brian stammered, still a little taken aback that Ferrer had picked up his phone. Ferrer asked what agency Brian was with, Brian told him the California Department of Justice, and Ferrer agreed to take the ad down and send Brian back-end information about the posting.

It was pretty simple, but it showed us that Ferrer was hands-on with the website and was accustomed to receiving calls from law enforcement agencies telling him that there were sex-trafficking ads on his website. He also sent an email to Brian to confirm that he had removed the ad. We now had Ferrer's email address, which was exactly what we needed to substantiate a specific location for the search warrant.

Our biggest break was learning that Google held Backpage's email servers. Ferrer's email address was managed by a Google business platform. Google is incorporated in California, so we had the advantage of being able to serve a search warrant without involving another state.

By this time, we had a lot of evidence. We had the unequivocal purpose of Backpage as a commercial sex hub, from the perspective both of girls sold and of all the buyers who called our officer. We had the communications with NCMEC. We had Brian's call and email with Ferrer himself. We had the NCMEC victims. And we had many, many reports from other law enforcement agencies and our own detailing ways in which victims were bought and sold using Backpage. We also collected all of the subpoenas from other law enforcement agencies to Backpage in sex-trafficking cases, which showed that Carl Ferrer was inundated, on a daily basis, with law enforcement requests for records related to sex-trafficking cases. If Ferrer printed out every advertisement selling a child for sex, he would have buried himself in paper. We finally had enough to show probable cause that a felony was being committed by Ferrer and that evidence of it would be in emails located at Google.

A Placer County judge signed off on the very first search warrant for Ferrer's emails.

Google was uncomfortable with our warrant, saying it was a huge swath of information to deliver. At that time, the warrant was sealed, and we were not required to provide notice to Ferrer that we were executing a warrant for his email. Google was obligated both to keep the warrant confidential and to turn over what it had despite its reservations.

Later, a California statute known as the California Electronic Communications Privacy Act (CalECPA) passed, requiring law enforcement to notify suspects when serving warrants to third parties, giving suspects an advantage, especially in white-collar investigations.[5] But an officer could include a sworn statement laying out a justification for delayed notification and attempt to buy extra time. Even if a judge granted delayed notification, the delay would need to be renewed and would eventually expire.

The new law hindered investigations. Once suspects know they are being investigated, it is harder to obtain evidence, identify victim assets in fraud cases, and stay ahead of fleeing suspects. It made longer, more complex investigations especially difficult. But it was a new California law that passed during the course of our investigation, and we had to learn to comply with it.

We were giddy when the package from Google arrived at the Department of Justice. It was just a yellow padded envelope containing a hard drive, but I could hardly wait to see what was inside. Before I or anyone from my team could delve in, the hard drive needed to be properly stored in evidence. The emails were downloaded into a searchable database and then searched for any emails that could involve the attorney-client privilege. The attorney-client privilege generally protects information from disclosure when it is between a person and his or her lawyer and relates to legal advice or future litigation. We were aware of an in-house attorney at Backpage, Liz McDougall, as well as several outside counsel that Backpage executives regularly consulted with. A separate "taint team" segregated any attorney emails into a separate locked file that no one investigating or prosecuting the case could look at. The role of a "taint team" is to ensure that the investigation is not tainted by any breach of attorney-client privilege. Some of the segregated emails would not necessarily be privileged—just because an email is to or from a lawyer does not render it privileged. But to be safe, we would segregate them all. This of course took weeks instead of days, as I impatiently and constantly checked in to see when we might be able to review the evidence.

After the emails were scrubbed for anything that could be attorney-client privilege, we finally got to review them. They showed who Ferrer was communicating with internally to run the operation as well as whom he was reporting to. It was clear that James Larkin and Mike Lacey, longtime founding owners, were still calling the shots.

Some of the emails included spreadsheet attachments. Once downloaded, they showed how much money Backpage was making. It was more than any of us had imagined: millions of dollars each month, just on sex ads in the female-escort section. We were only focused on California, as we only had jurisdiction over California transactions, and were trying to figure out what money came from where. We learned that the defendants operated mainly out of a headquarters office in Dallas, Texas, with another major office in Arizona. Unless the victim posted an ad in California or we could otherwise connect the defendants and their crimes to California, we would not be able to prove that we had jurisdiction. But we were able to divide the ads by city, choosing the largest California cites to analyze.

We also quickly determined that over 90–100 percent of Backpage's monthly revenue was from the escort section, not the furniture, car, or other sections.[6] It appeared that Ferrer was emailing back and forth with other advertisers to buy bulk advertisements in order to populate other sections of the site. But unlike the escort section, he was not investing in driving traffic to those areas of the site. They were merely a shell. It also appeared that Ferrer was emailing with Lacey and Larkin to provide regular updates about the company, growth strategy, legal and political concerns, and bottom-line financials. Larkin and Lacey would respond with questions, ideas, sometimes jokes.

Larkin, Lacey, and Ferrer were all well aware of Backpage's role in sex trafficking. Using the search terms "sex trafficking" and "human trafficking" and "child sex" resulted in thousands of emails in which they discussed how to respond to criticism about their role in child sex trafficking, how to work with other major corporations that were wary of them because of their role in sex trafficking, and whether and when to prevent certain pictures from being allowed on their site.

With that evidence, we drafted a new search warrant with a more extensive list of email accounts in a longer date range. We now needed the email accounts of Larkin and Lacey and others whom Ferrer was regularly corresponding with to run what was more clearly looking like a criminal enterprise. The Placer County judge signed off, and we went back to Google with the more extensive warrant. Google lawyers raised their eyebrows at us, but after some wrangling, they ended up giving us the evidence we were entitled to. This took months, and more months, to scrub for attorney-client privilege and download into our searchable database.

From the new accounts, we extracted even more evidence, including more details about the financial workings of the company. We now had a database with millions of emails, and it was overwhelming. I was the only lawyer, and Brian was the only dedicated agent. We were drowning in evidence.

As a prosecutor, under California law, you are obligated to make every piece of evidence available to the defense, even if it was theirs to begin with. Under constitutional law, you are required to ensure that any evidence that could be considered exculpatory to the defendant is shared with the defense. This is known as the *Brady* rule.[7] At the end of the day, you are seeking to convict a defendant of a crime, something that will probably take away his or her freedom and greatly alter his or her life. The critical check on the prosecutor's power in the justice system is the ability of the defendant to have an attorney represent him or her, and that attorney must have the ability to view all evidence, especially evidence that could be favorable, in order to do his or her job.

Moreover, as the prosecutor, it is critical to review all facts, to seek out all evidence, and to persistently search for the truth. This is a principle that exists for every case, no matter what the circumstances are and no matter what you think the defendant did and how horrible he or she is. So not only would I need to review this material meticulously, but I would also need to figure out how to make it accessible to the defense team, if I ever charged the case. I was cruising forward and building a solid case, but it was abundantly clear that we needed more help.

Most days, it felt like me against the world. Backpage was one of several major cases I was juggling, and I was still trying to build out a statewide human-trafficking team. I would sometimes talk to Dave Druliner, my longtime DOJ mentor and friend, but what I was trying to do was even beyond anything he'd tried.

Then Dave was diagnosed with cancer. He was semiretired while going through a series of treatments. He remained optimistic and never let the pain show, but he was fighting for his life. I savored the time I had with him. We had traditionally gone to breakfast every Friday morning as a way to stay in touch when I was in my new unit. He insisted on ordering me bacon every time. We continued the tradition when he left DOJ to focus on his health, saying our work together kept him young. I still greatly valued his advice on my cases and genuinely enjoyed his company. Now his stories were about the ladies at the nursing facility where he was recovering and how he crashed a car three times in two days and could no longer be trusted with driving.

I hadn't heard from Dave in a few weeks when his daughter told me to come see him one day in the fall. It would be my last visit with him, and I treasured it greatly. He told me that he had taught me everything he knew and that he was so proud of me. He told me that if anyone could take down Backpage, it was me. And he told me to teach what he taught me to the next generation of great prosecutors. He spread out his hand as if to signify the importance of spreading knowledge and bringing up the new prosecutors to do things the right way. He told me he was satisfied. Dave died the day after that visit.

As a prosecutor, I had been exposed to the tragedy of death many times. I met with a mom who held out hope that her son who had been missing for nearly twenty years was still alive, to tell her I was prosecuting the man who murdered him. I consoled the mom of a teenage murder victim who would have given anything to hug him one more time and run her fingers through his wavy brown hair. And I held the hand of my close friend, another prosecutor, as she learned her two-and-a-half-year-old daughter had been murdered by her abusive ex.

I was never one to take my life or anyone else's for granted and knew all too well from the cases I worked around, and my own tragic experiences, that aging is a privilege. I was grateful I had the chance to say good-bye to Dave. And now, his words, "if anyone can do this, it's you," would be the rallying cry I needed to push the Backpage case forward.

6

RUNNING OUT OF TIME

FINALLY had a meeting set up in November 2015 with the attorney general's executive team in San Francisco. Jessica Owen, the fairly new attorney who was prosecuting Andrew Jordan with me, was smart, hardworking, and very interested in the Backpage case. Although she worked in another unit in Los Angeles, she found ways to make time for the case and convince her supervisors that it was a worthy endeavor. She was a great asset in helping me review the vast email info-dump and would be accompanying me to the meeting in San Francisco.

It was only a couple of weeks after Dave had died. I wished I could have called him on the drive from Sacramento to San Francisco to run through my case presentation. Better yet, I wished we were driving together, practicing at a Taco Bell, and tag-teaming the meeting. He was perfect in those sorts of meetings. He had such an impressive presence, and no one dared challenge him. But it would just be Jessica and me. And I was struggling to take the enormous space that he once filled.

The goal was for the attorney general's team to applaud the prosecution, give us additional resources, and give approval to file the case. "Great job, Maggy. Tell us what resources you need to get this filed," is what I wanted to hear.

I practiced a dramatic opening statement a million times on the drive to San Francisco. I described the Backpage owners as a new breed of slave traders:

In 1865, the Thirteenth Amendment to the United States Constitution sought to abolish slavery. Yet today, a new and horrifying kind of slavery is seeping into the back pages of our society: child sex trafficking. Young girls are forced into abusive and coercive situations where they are obligated to perform degrading sexual acts in exchange for sustenance.

This is a case about a new generation of slave traders who have created an online marketplace to exploit the most vulnerable people in our society, all while pocketing millions and millions of dollars each month.

The website is called Backpage.com, and each day it operates in eight hundred cities across the world and sells thousands and thousands of people. You will hear that the defendants, Carl Ferrer, James Larkin, and Mike Lacey, created Backpage for the purpose of capitalizing on the prostitution industry despite its illegality and despite the devastating effect it's had on children and human-trafficking victims.

In my mind, the case was emotionally compelling, intellectually impressive, and close to being ready to be filed. Most cases did not require approval from the attorney general herself, but a case of this magnitude needed to go through executive screening, be approved by several layers of management, and ultimately be signed off by Attorney General Harris. I knew that I still had work to do, but I wanted filing approval in advance so that I could start putting the pieces in place, garner more resources, and have credibility when working with other agencies that would ask about the status of the case. I wanted to wow the executive team so that they would assign additional agents to the case and make it a top priority for the attorney general. I at least thought they would give me the green light to move forward.

They didn't. They were confused and had a lot of questions and concerns. Why weren't the feds doing such a big case? How had we gotten involved? *Why* had we gotten involved? And how could we possibly show the defendants' specific knowledge about our individual victims when there were hundreds of people sold each night? How could we overcome the immunity granted by the Communications Decency Act? Could filing this case backfire?

Granted, these were special assistants to the attorney general. They weren't prosecutors. They were smart and worked their tails off and were politically savvy, but they did not have experience with prosecuting a criminal case or what human trafficking really looked like.

We walked through the case in detail again. We answered all their questions. We explained the case law on specific intent, what evidence we had for each charge, and our legal strategies for overcoming the CDA. The team said that they'd brief the attorney general and that we should keep working, but we did not have approval to charge the case.

I drove home, stuck in traffic and frustrated. Why was I unable to convince them that this case needed to be filed and that it needed to be filed immediately? I had met the burden of proof hundreds of times in other cases I'd charged and prosecuted. Why did this case seem so insurmountable to everyone?

THE FBI

By the time I got back to Sacramento, it was after 6:00 p.m. My phone rang just as I pulled into my driveway. It was a blocked number. I was accustomed to picking up blocked calls, as they were usually from Reye or Brian, and I expected one of them to be calling me back so that I could vent about my horrible meeting with the executive team and the ensuing four hours of traffic. But this was a different voice. It was an FBI agent from a San Diego task force, one that our office ran and that I had helped set up. I had never met this particular agent, Jeff, and he was furious at me. I should not have picked up the call. I should have already been with my husband and kids inside, either playing Mario Kart with Ben or heading out to shoot hoops with Tyler or stealing jambalaya from the delicious pot Cary was making for

Friday-night dinner. But there I was in the driveway embroiled with Jeff.

He was accusing me of interfering with an investigation because I had requested an interview with a minor who was in custody in San Diego. She was a missing child reported to NCMEC and was being sold on Backpage. Jeff was working on some other case that she was involved in. I told him that I could wait to interview her and that my interview questions were very limited, that I would not jeopardize his investigation. I even offered to let him sit in on any interview that I did. This did not assuage his unfounded concerns. He asked what I was doing to deconflict, the process that law enforcement uses to ensure that a case they are investigating isn't already being investigated by another agency. I explained that her name was not associated with any FBI case, based on information from his own field office. The truth was that he hadn't entered her information into the system, and so there was no way I could have known about his case. He claimed that she was a victim in a larger case, was uncooperative, and was doing time on her own case, which he would not provide information on. I asked him about his own methodology, why she was in custody, and whether she was receiving trauma-informed care. This angered him. How dare I ask any questions about his protocol? What was the point of this Backpage investigation anyway? It was going nowhere, he assumed.

And therein was the heart of the problem—two problems, actually. First, law enforcement was still treating sex-trafficking victims like criminals. Second, the FBI's lack of enthusiasm for our case was making things harder.

At that time, law enforcement's practice was to arrest underage girls for prostitution, even though they were not legally capable of consent and were statutory-rape victims and sex-trafficking victims as well. Sacramento was no different. Juvenile hall was full of sex-trafficking victims. Worse, traffickers often used juvenile hall to recruit. Girls in custody would convince other girls in custody to come work with them when they got out. It was a vicious cycle.

It's not that the officers ever wanted to incarcerate kids. But sometimes there wasn't really a good choice. The victims, or defendants, were chronic runaways with pages of warrants for a variety of offenses. Many times these offenses relate to being a trafficking victim—shoplifting, drugs, absconding from placement centers such as group homes—but an officer probably would not know that on first encounter, and there weren't many options. These kids ran away from home, ran away from nonsecure placement centers, and were a danger to themselves. The officers reasoned that at least juvenile hall provided a safe place, off the streets, access to medical care, and full meals.

But it was still jail. Moreover, it was still force and coercion but only by another name. How could we deprive a young person of her freedom merely to protect her from being deprived of her freedom by a trafficker? It couldn't possibly be right. But the lack of alternatives was stifling. There was a rotation of nonprofits that were overwhelmed and understaffed. There were group homes that seemed to serve as sex-trafficking recruitment grounds, and there were relatives whom victims ran away from again and again.

It is heartbreaking to see, but even after law enforcement intervention, most victims return to their traffickers or find new traffickers or sell their bodies on their own. Sometimes, after several interventions and the right combination of support and services, victims overcome their trauma to live healthy, successful, and meaningful lives. But it is a journey, and it takes time—much longer than it takes to prosecute a typical case.

Meanwhile, I was running out of time and being pulled in a million directions. I was the statewide human-trafficking coordinator and now a supervising deputy attorney general over the Special Crimes Unit. We prosecuted corruption cases and financial-crime cases, and I had new attorneys to train. But all I wanted to do was close my office door and draft criminal charges against Backpage.

Attorney General Kamala Harris was talking about human trafficking frequently; she had said she wanted to kill Backpage. Yet I still didn't feel as if I had the support to bring it down, and I was tasked with so many other cases. We had occasional help from local law enforcement agencies. But often they were funded by FBI task forces, and I still didn't have the FBI's buy-in, as evinced by my call with Jeff.

Backpage was a prolific source of information for law enforcement. We used it to locate victims and as evidence against pimps. If Backpage closed, the FBI was concerned it would have dozens of little sites to monitor, and those little sites might be uncooperative and offshore. I understood this concern, but when your snitch is the biggest criminal in the ring, at some point you have to stop turning a blind eye. And what the FBI didn't seem to understand was that Backpage wasn't fully cooperating. Sure, it responded quickly to subpoenas, but it didn't provide all the information it could. It didn't provide rejected ads or metadata or any of the type of evidence that law enforcement could use to really get in front of the problem. Backpage did just enough to placate authorities while not undermining its own bottom line.

I scheduled a sit-down meeting with the FBI and US Attorney's Office. First, I didn't want to piss off anyone else. I just wanted to move the case forward, and I needed help. We needed to set up some guardrails so that the feds would be at least comfortable with our investigation, even if they could not support it. Second, the case was only getting bigger, and in my mind, it was a case the feds should consider prosecuting.

The meeting seemed productive. The chiefs said that they would make sure the field offices cooperated with our investigation, and we even signed a memorandum of understanding to work together. This agreement at least eased the tension at the field level and put the case on the agencies' radar. I hoped that eventually the feds would make a case.

But in the meantime, we continued to build our state case, executing additional search warrants and organizing information piece by piece. We had amassed millions of pages of data and earned the trust and cooperation of victims throughout the state. At this point, I was satisfied that we could prove that the defendants had the requisite knowledge and criminal intent, but because of the Communications Decency Act, we also had to prepare for the website immunity defense. They would claim that because the advertisements were being placed by a third party, they could not be held criminally responsible for what transpired from them. In addition to preparing to prove that they were accepting money, conduct, and not speech, I wanted to show that they were assisting in creating the content itself, which would make them ineligible for the CDA immunity defense altogether.

To that end, we discovered other websites owned by the suspects—websites purchased to kill off the competition and drive all the commercial-sex advertising to their sites. For example, Backpage owned websites called EvilEmpire and Big City. It used these websites to cross-promote the Backpage ads, draw more traffic to Backpage, and corner the market. In one email exchange between Ferrer and one of his top employees, Ferrer sent a list of possible competition websites. They were discussing how to kill the other websites and purchase additional URLs. "We do this better than anyone any day of the week," the email said. In order to populate EvilEmpire and Big City, the defendants would use information from Backpage ads and rearrange it. In other words, they were creating their own ads using the victims' information. In another email, a user asked Backpage to take down her ad on EvilEmpire. The Backpage employee denied any knowledge of or affiliation with the site.

This not only bolstered evidence of the suspects' knowledge but also went toward content creation. If we could show that the suspects were creating content, they would no longer be protected by the CDA. The fact that they created other websites on which no one except them could post or remove ads went to show that they were at least creating content for these auxiliary sites and potentially violating the victims' rights over their own images.

We also saw emails back and forth about their "moderation" practices in which they discussed saving deleted ads and allowing users to repost sanitized versions of the ads. Essentially, Backpage staff was being trained to assist traffickers in posting ads of victims without alerting law enforcement. Deleted ads were kept, potentially for some other site Backpage was creating, but never shared with law enforcement.

Backpage staff was directing users on how to post and helping to post. In some instances, moderators would delete offensive words or pictures and post the ads. The third parties were not creating the ads on their own—Backpage had a hand, at least in part, in creating the ads.

Backpage also kept lists of its most frequent users: sex traffickers who advertised multiple women in multiple cities and gang members who sold children online. Staff would reach out to these users to offer specials, credits, and ways to use Bitcoin. Anyone who was posting ads in multiple cities, using several phone numbers and a rotation of invasive pictures of sexualized teenage girls, was not a commercial sex worker trying to make ends meet. These were sex traffickers, and Ferrer, Larkin, and Lacey were partnering with them.

We were also able to track Ferrer buying the company from Larkin and Lacey, at least on paper. This appeared to be a way to manipulate the company's assets and for Larkin and Lacey to at least appear out of the business. It was another evasion technique. But based on other documents and records, it was clear that Larkin and Lacey had essentially given Ferrer a high-interest loan for a purchase of the company that was really just a sham—Larkin and Lacey were still the biggest financial beneficiaries and received almost all of the company's profits.

In addition to monitoring the suspects' business activity, we were also trying to preserve data. Backpage could disappear any day, and we'd be left with nothing to show. They seemed to be moving the company offshore piece by piece. Ferrer was renting office space in the Netherlands and going to meetings all over Europe. If they got wind of our investigation, they could move the entire operation overseas and stop hosting ads in US cities. A partial shutdown would be a step in the right direction, but at this point, I also wanted to bring them to justice. The clock was ticking. I was still waiting for the green light to prosecute, but I thought the case was getting close.

MORE VICTIMS

We continued to refine our strategy, meeting with more victims. Carissa or another victim advocate accompanied us. We met with Lizzie, the little sister of Kim, whom we had met during our very first sting operation using the Thorn data. She described the way that Backpage normalized sex trafficking. She thought that if there was something wrong with it, posting an ad would not be so easy right there on the internet. She said that she had never had an ad rejected, even though some of her ads said, "16 and sweet." She said that at first it was fun—she had freedom, money, attention. Everyone wanted her, she recalled. And then one night she was brutally gang raped and nobody cared. She was alone sobbing and bleeding in an empty hotel bathtub, and nobody even checked on her. The next day she was back out on the street working. "That's the life," she recalled gloomily. But it was no way to live—it was a path to death. We tried to help her as best we could. Lizzie wanted to be kept up-to-date on the progress of our case. She felt duped by Backpage and saw the connection between the site and her suffering. She felt ready to move forward with her own life, and being part of this case was an important step for her.

I tried to interview the victims in ways that empowered them, rather than making them feel like they were being questioned or did something wrong. Another victim, Drea, was also sixteen years old when we met. She came to the Attorney General's Office to meet me, but the conference room was booked: Robert Morgester was sitting in there with guys in suits, and I couldn't interrupt. So I walked her down the hall to my office, a messy desk with several half-full Starbucks cups, four chairs, and a great view of the Sacramento skyline. I asked her which chair she wanted, and she took mine, behind the messy desk. There she was, swiveling around in my spot and gazing out the office window. "You look like a lawyer," I said. "Maybe someday," she giggled. "I'll save you this office," I said.

As a prosecutor, there are limits on the relationships you can build with victims. For one, you can never have a substantive conversation with a victim or witness without an officer present, as it would then turn the prosecutor into a witness. You also must report any conversations you have with a witness to the defense, and so you need an officer or some other individual to create that report. Once I bought a pizza for a victim in a child-abuse case—and promptly disclosed this to the defense—and the defense attorney tried to make it sound like I was bribing her to testify. "And Ms. Krell bought you a pizza and gave you money for video games, didn't she? And then she told you to answer her questions?" It was ridiculous—and funny when the witness responded, "Who's Ms. Krell?" Defense lawyer: "This prosecutor sitting at this table," pointing at me. Witness: "Oh, you mean Maggy." But the point is that there are professional boundaries because the victims should not have any allegiance to the prosecutor. Their only obligation is to tell the truth. So as much as I personally wanted to do for these victims, my role was to prosecute the case, and I didn't want to create any sense that they were somehow beholden to me or that I would help them in some way. But we're not robots, and humanity and compassion must prevail over the rigid confines of our roles. I had an opportunity, an inroad into people's lives often at the most challenging of times. And I could perhaps subtly leave Drea with a vision and hope for herself that maybe she hadn't fully realized before. It starts with having someone believe in your future and empowering you to make decisions, even if they are just little decisions like where to sit in an office.

We tried to bring in victims from across the state, to show that this was not just a Sacramento or even a Northern California case; it was the entire state. In reality, it was the entire nation and even the entire world. But we needed jurisdiction in California, and this was our focus. With help from local law enforcement, we were still working on tracking down sex-trafficking victims in multiple states who had been sold in California. NCMEC would send us missing persons reports, and we would work with local agencies to try and piece together who and where these victims were.

There was one picture with two girls: a seventeen-year-old named Leslie and a thirteen-year-old named Shyla. I was able to obtain police reports involving their cases and learned that Leslie, now an adult, was being sentenced on a criminal case of her own. She had been charged with trafficking Shyla. Leslie had recruited Shyla, taught her the "rules of the game," and refused to testify against their trafficker when law enforcement finally intervened. They were advertised together as a "two-girl special," "young and fresh," and almost nude, posed provocatively on a hotel bed near Los Angeles. There was no way anyone could look at Shyla and not see a child, a scared little girl.

We wanted to talk with Shyla and see if she could be part of our case. We sent letters to her mom, went to her multiple addresses, checked with district schools, but could not find a trace of her anywhere. We learned from local law enforcement that she disappeared soon after her trafficker had been arrested. We continued to see her picture pop up on Backpage, even though Backpage had been notified that she was a thirteen-year-old sex-trafficking victim. She appeared to be for sale in LA and Vegas and Oakland. But when we called the number on the ad to try and set up a "date" with Shyla, it was never really her. We never found Shyla.

We did find Leslie. She was on the path to healing. Her sentence was being served at a residential treatment program where she sobered up and enrolled in cosmetology school. She was willing to testify in our case and welcomed the opportunity to tell her tragic and unfair story. And she told us about Shyla. Shyla was a runaway whose mom was incarcerated. She never met her dad. Leslie had taken Shyla under her wing and provided for her as best she could. But she did it the only way she knew how—through prostitution. She never had to force Shyla. Shyla wanted to be like Leslie. She wanted to make her own money. She wanted to wear heels and makeup and look pretty and get attention.

But neither Leslie nor Shyla really ever had their own money. They were both working for Leslie's "boyfriend." He was a seasoned street trafficker who housed several girls at a time. He helped them recruit buyers using Backpage, provided security, and kept most of the profits. He supplied the house with drugs, alcohol, occasional meals, and fresh clothing. Leslie said that after Shyla's first night "making money," he took them both shopping, but nothing in the adult section fit Shyla. Leslie never wanted to turn on her boyfriend because he took care of them. They would have been homeless without him, she thought.

Leslie acknowledged the role that Backpage played in her exploitation. She didn't think she would have been able to do it without Backpage. She would never just stand on a street corner, she said. She said that after her ads went stale, Backpage would email her, offering free ads and then charging her for premium placement. She said this kept her going, even when she was thinking of getting out. She said she used commercial-sex proceeds to buy more ads. This was essential to proving that the defendants were committing the California crime of pimping—receiving the earnings of commercial sex in whole or in part.

Reye and I went to LA to meet with a victim named Michelle. She was sixteen years old and had been advertised on Backpage in San Francisco, Los Angeles, and San Diego. In San Diego, she was caught up in a sting. Law enforcement called the number on her ad, met with her at a hotel, and identified her as a missing child. Even after Backpage was notified and she went home to her family, we continued to see her ads surface throughout California.

Reye and I were accompanied by a victim advocate with the Los Angeles County District Attorney's Office. The advocate had worked with Michelle on a case against the street trafficker who had been pimping her out. She had established a strong rapport with Michelle and offered to join us so that the interview would be more comfortable. We met the advocate at a Starbucks near Michelle's family home. The advocate had a teddy bear with her that she said was a gift for Michelle. I remember thinking it was odd for the advocate to be bringing this victim, whom I perceived as a grown women, a teddy bear. I had only seen her picture on Backpage. She looked like she could be in her twenties wearing huge hoop earrings, long manicured nails, and a tight black dress. But when we got to Michelle's house, we were visiting a scared child wearing pink pajama pants and a Micky Mouse tank top. And she loved the teddy bear.

Michelle described the way her Backpage ads generated business for her "boyfriend." Like many victims, Michelle would never describe him as a "pimp" or "trafficker." She would post an ad and immediately receive calls. Her boyfriend would drive her to various locations and wait outside. Before the police sting, she had been sexually assaulted and beaten in a hotel room in San Diego. She was scared and just wanted to go home. She stated that she didn't know why her picture was still on Backpage.

Reye had a word with Michelle's dad. You could see pain and brokenness in his eyes. He told Reye that she still frequently ran away and that he suspected she was having sex for money but he felt helpless and did not know what to do. The victim advocate offered several victim services in the LA area.

Michelle's dad made an impression on Reye, who had two teenage daughters of his own. Reye was a doting and dedicated father but nevertheless felt the vulnerabilities that we all feel as parents.

After meeting with victims like Leslie and Michelle, we would have to locate their Backpage advertisement and transaction details. We needed to show that Backpage received money from them. This often meant sending Backpage a search warrant for their ads. We had to show the transaction record: how much had they paid Backpage, when had it taken place, how many times the ad had been posted or reposted, how many financial transactions we could identify. Backpage, not realizing that our inquiry was related to an investigation of the company, supplied the transaction information. If it didn't show that the ad was purchased or it did not occur within the requisite time period or it was not in California, we couldn't use it. The information Backpage supplied was limited. I knew we needed to figure out how to pull its transaction records, which were probably stored in some cloud or on some server at its headquarters in Texas.

I continued to build an arsenal of survivors who were willing to testify. Some of them even felt empowered by it. I knew all too well from prosecuting domestic violence cases and other sex-trafficking cases that testifying in court is often the last thing victims want. I did not want to dredge up traumatic memories for victims who were trying to leave them behind or force victims to share experiences that they were still ashamed by. But to my relief, and thanks to Carissa and other victim advocates, survivors were reaching out to me voluntarily. It was challenging to find their old Backpage ads, but at least I had their stories. They wanted to know when the case was being filed. And as the investigation kept dragging on, more and more new kids were being sold on Backpage.

There were also victims whose murders were enabled through Backpage. We reviewed records involving four young women advertised on Backpage and then found murdered in Detroit in 2011. Faced with criticism and potential liability, Backpage executives scrambled to craft a media strategy in which they blamed other websites even though those websites received the advertisement from Backpage. There were cases in New Orleans, Dallas, Scottsdale, Detroit, and Chicago in which young women trafficked on Backpage were killed, and yet the site continued to expand and the owners continued to profit.

In the ensuing months, every so often, I'd get follow-up questions from the attorney general's executive team. I'd submit a memo answering the questions. And then I wouldn't hear anything for weeks. It was not clear whether they had substantive concerns about the case or whether the attorney general just didn't have time to consider it yet. I truthfully did not know whether she had actually been briefed. All I could do was keep building the case, keep answering their questions, and do my best to move us forward.

I knew we needed an ironclad case; we had to think through every possible claim the defense could raise, so that we could respond persuasively. Like every case, defendants are innocent until and unless proven guilty. But every day, every night, more teenagers were sold for sex on Backpage, the owners made more money, and the chances of our investigation attracting their notice increased. The victims we'd identified early on were in the wind, and for some, the statute of limitations had already ended.

Time was running out.

7

FLIGHT 21

BY 2016, all around the country, more states were starting to focus on tackling human trafficking. As I was trying to get a dedicated unit in California, a colleague sent me an article about a new unit that was being formed in Texas. The lead attorney was named Kirsta Melton. I decided to reach out and call her, knowing that Backpage was based in Texas and that every sex-trafficking prosecutor knows about Backpage. I introduced myself and congratulated her on her new position. We talked about the kinds of trends we were seeing in our respective states: the growing involvement of gangs in the human-trafficking trade and the lack of resources for victims. As it turned out, we were living parallel lives halfway across the country! We were both busy moms scrambling to get our kids to sports practices and games while also prosecuting some of the most depraved criminals in our respective states. We both struggled with internal politics at our organizations and could commiserate about the lack of law enforcement resources dedicated to combating human trafficking. And above all else, we were both hell-bent on helping kids and doing everything we could to disrupt sex trafficking. Eventually, I confided in her about our Backpage investigation. As far as I knew, it was the only such investigation in the country.

Kirsta was immediately excited about the prospect of taking down Backpage. She and her team agreed to help with anything we needed, including arrests if the defendants were in Texas. And they promised they would help us execute a search of the Backpage headquarters in Dallas. They started their own investigation, and we agreed to share information. Kirsta and her team even came out to California a couple of times to review evidence and strategize with us. She had big hair, a Texas twang, and a similar passion for the case. It was great having her as a thought-partner. And it crossed my mind that if I never got approval to file this case, at least Texas could prosecute them. . . .

I was working around the clock. I would go out with friends to blow off steam and still couldn't stop talking about Backpage. My two dear girlfriends Lorena Moya and Kate Wheatley spent many margaritas and baskets of chips hearing about "the internet case," as they called it. But despite not knowing about sex trafficking or criminal prosecutions, their reaction was clear: How could these men possibly get away with this? Why should someone be able to do something on a website that they couldn't do on a street corner? It was so plain to anyone who would listen, and I couldn't wait to explain it to a jury.

Yiota from NCMEC would call periodically and ask if I had any news. I told her we were close, but I had been saying that for so long that it had lost its meaning. Carissa and I would check in every now and then; she would give me updates on victims she was in touch with and remind me that everyone was counting on me. I always reassured her that we were still on track.

But I still didn't have the green light from Attorney General Harris, and I was mired in other cases. After finishing a contentious fraud trial, my family and I went on a badly needed vacation. It was July, and we would be celebrating my son Tyler's ninth birthday. We went to one of our favorite places in the world, Truckee, California. Tyler and his seven-year-old brother, Ben, were avid crawdad catchers. Cary and I would picnic together on the shores of Donner Lake, taking in picture-perfect mountain views while the kids would dangle chicken bones into the water while perched on a large bolder. They would emerge with delightful clawed critters, which they'd observe in a bucket before releasing at dusk, and even bigger smiles.

One afternoon, Tyler and I were kayaking on Donner Lake. It happened to be a Tuesday, but for my purposes, it was still Saturday—I was officially on vacation. I had brought my cell phone in a plastic bag so that we could take pictures. Tyler noticed my phone was ringing, but I ignored it. But it kept ringing, and then I saw that I was getting text messages from the chief deputy attorney general.

I picked up. It was Attorney General Harris, with questions about Backpage. The phone kept cutting out. There I was in the middle of a lake, trying not to tip a small boat or drop a paddle, while answering questions from the attorney general about the most important case in the history of the world.

The attorney general rarely calls. The last time she called me, I'd been in a bowling alley. I had a well-established pattern of having the most important people call at the worst possible times, and this might have been the most extreme example. While holding the phone with my ear and shoulder, I feverishly paddled back to the dock, jumped out, left Tyler, and sprinted up the road to get some semblance of cell reception.

Attorney General Harris was talking quickly and intensely, and I could only understand every third word. She was asking if we could charge possession of child pornography and how many estimated child victims I thought there were. She had prosecuted sex crimes, fought for children's rights, and wanted to kill Backpage as badly as I did. But true to her reputation, she had her own thoughts, and she was grilling me.

From the top of the road, overlooking Donner Lake, slightly out of breath, I explained the case to her. I explained that we had been working it for over two years, that we had identified and had reports for over one hundred California children who had been trafficked multiple times on Backpage, that we had survivors ready and willing to testify, and that this case would change the world.

I also laid out the challenges. I predicted we'd be up against dozens of high-powered lawyers but promised we wouldn't be outmatched. I told her that there were real legal issues, that we were breaking ground on new theories around the CDA that might not hold up. But at the end of the day, I told her, this is a righteous case, we have a good-faith belief we will convict these defendants, and who are we if don't file it? Before we hung up, she said, "Go get 'em."

My heart was still pumping as I sprinted back down to the dock and realized that my son had floated into the middle of the lake and that I would be swimming to the kayak with the phone held above my head! We enjoyed the rest of our vacation, knowing I'd be busier than ever when I returned.

GO TIME

Shortly after I got back from Truckee, in August 2016, I needed to go to Long Beach to go to trial on the Jordan case. This was the one I had dismissed on the eve of trial at the end of the previous year, and there was no way I was getting any more time. I needed to get that case done before I could do the Backpage arrests. I would also be showing Jessica Owen the ropes on her very first trial and hopefully convicting a violent and manipulative defendant of sex trafficking. It was an important case for many reasons and especially for Alicia and Tasha, who would be mustering the courage to testify. I had spoken with them and their tireless victim advocate over the previous several months as they went through fear, depression, and anxiety. They would be facing their abuser in court, an act of extraordinary courage.

While I was in Long Beach in trial, I was also orchestrating the details of the Backpage arrest operation with Kirsta in Texas. After delivering closing argument, I flew home, leaving Jessica and Detective Chris Zamora to languish over the jury's deliberations. They had both done an amazing job with this case, but Jessica was understandably nervous. Not me. I was confident the jury would do the right thing. Fletcher had become unhinged throughout the proceedings—he bullied Alicia and Tasha, just as his client had, and it only made them more sympathetic. As horrible as it was to watch, I believed it would result in a conviction. Meanwhile, the day I'd dreamed about for years was fast approaching. We were finally bringing down Carl Ferrer, and I had zero space in my brain to worry about what Jordan's jury was worrying about.

Back in Sacramento, Special Agent Brian Fichtner and I threw ourselves into final planning. Brian was an easygoing, roll-with-the-punches guy—kind, thoughtful, and humble. He never in his life expected to be orchestrating the biggest sex-trafficking bust in history, but that's what we were trying to do. We needed to draft three bulletproof arrest warrants, execute those warrants in multiple states with the help of multiple law enforcement agencies, and search and seize vital documents from Backpage's Dallas headquarters.

Every part of the plan had to happen discreetly, flawlessly, and as close to simultaneously as possible. If one or more of our suspects got wind of what was happening, they might alert the others and flee the country, destroying incriminating evidence along the way.

As Brian and I went over the many moving pieces, plugging holes and gaming out scenarios, I had moments of panic. Ferrer, Larkin, and Lacey would have every financial and legal resource at their disposal to crush this prosecution. I was a state prosecutor who had to beg, borrow, and barter assistance anywhere I could. What made me think I could pull this off?

But I thought about the bravery of the survivors in sharing their traumatic stories and my conversation with Carissa nearly three years earlier in the conference room on the ninth floor of the Attorney General's Office. There was even a sticky note still attached to my sliding keyboard shelf with the three goals: shut down the site, felony conviction, fix the CDA. I made a promise. It was time to keep it.

Brian and I started with the warrants, which would be accompanied by a criminal complaint. An arrest warrant provides facts sufficient to allow a court to find probable cause that a suspect committed a crime. Most warrants are brief and straightforward, especially when accompanied with a charging document. A warrant could be written on a cocktail napkin, as long as it identifies the subject, articulates facts, and specifies a crime.

Not this time. Carl Ferrer's arrest warrant needed to be a work of art. We knew that thousands of people would read the warrants, and hundreds of lawyers would pore over each and every word. We wanted to use them to tell the story of the countless women and children whose lives had been destroyed because of Backpage. We wanted to describe the downward spiral of their self-esteem and their health: the times they went to jail, the times they were beaten and left for dead, the times their parents couldn't find them, the times their parents never looked. We wanted to tell the world about Drea and Leslie and Shyla and Kim and Lizzie and all of the other teenagers we had met with over the past two and half years, whose childhoods had been robbed. We also wanted to tell the story of the defendants, Ferrer, Larkin, and Lacey, greedy men who jetted around the world on the backs of these victims. We wanted to show that they knew their website incited rape and torture and even murder and that *they didn't care*. We wanted to use the warrants to show them that someone *did* care and that they were going to be held accountable for what they'd done.

Meanwhile, Jessica called with the Jordan verdicts: guilty on all counts. We were ecstatic. I spoke with both Alicia and Tasha. The criminal justice system had once again delivered vindication. The jury's verdict signified that twelve strangers believed Alicia and Tasha and cared about what happened to them. The verdict signified that it wasn't their fault. They didn't deserve what Jordan did to them. And they didn't have to be afraid of Jordan anymore—he'd be spending the next twenty-one years in prison for two counts of sex trafficking, pimping, and assault.

Brian and I revised and revised the warrants until we could revise no more. Then Brian took them to the Sacramento County courthouse for signing. There are dozens of judges in that big gray building, but only a few are on warrant duty at any given time.

Whom you get is the luck of the draw. Some judges nitpick you to death about typos and grammar. Others are inquisitive, seeming to want to try the case right there. Others just flip the pages and sign.

Which judge would we get? I paced my office, unable to make a dent in my mountainous workload. A few blocks away, Brian sat and stared at a wall, waiting for the judge to call him to chambers. His phone was switched off, so I couldn't pester him for updates—and he couldn't distract himself with Words with Friends.

I was on the phone with Reye Diaz, who was complaining about his role in the upcoming operation, when I finally got a text from Brian, reading, "I feel like I'm holding three winning lotto tickets!" The judge signed the warrants! He set bail and granted us authorization to arrest all three defendants, when and if we could find them.

That was a big "if." We had been working with Homeland Security for months to track the whereabouts of Ferrer, Lacey, and Larkin. There never seemed to be a week when they were all in the same country, let alone the same state! We prioritized arresting Ferrer, since as far as we could tell, he was closest to Backpage's daily operations and probably had the most information. We knew that he was in the Netherlands and that he had purchased a return ticket to Houston that would land on October 6, 2016.

So began step two of our massive operation. We dispatched law enforcement teams to carry out surveillance on two California residences owned by Larkin. Reye was assigned to travel to Arizona with Jessica Owen, who was fresh off the Jordan guilty verdicts and happy to rejoin the Backpage team. They would coordinate with local law enforcement and FBI agents in Arizona, who were helping locate Lacey, who had a residence in the state, and possibly Larkin, who also owned a house in Arizona. We had also discussed searching their Arizona offices but ultimately did not have the bandwidth to pull that off.

Brian and I went home, said good-bye to our families, and headed to the Sacramento airport. We were flying to Texas to execute the most difficult and critical steps in the plan: getting Ferrer and preserving evidence. We would be flying to Dallas together, but after Brian and I briefed the Texas teams, I would stay to help with the search of the Dallas headquarters while Brian would take a flight to Houston to pick up Ferrer.

On the way, I obsessively reviewed our strategy. Our best bet was to arrest Ferrer as soon as he got off the plane, then immediately give our fellow agents the go-ahead to arrest his coconspirators. But if Ferrer heard anything suspicious or if Larkin or Lacey realized they were being surveilled, Ferrer might not return to the United States. There was also a chance he would change his plans for totally unrelated reasons.

Adding another layer of complication, we had to depend on Texas to execute the warrant, as we had no authority to execute warrants outside California. We were at the mercy of other agencies, with their own priorities and resource constraints. Kirsta was moving heaven and earth to make it work, but she had her own internal challenges and a full caseload of her own. October 6 was the day. We were so close, but there were still so many ways it could all go wrong.

Still, my mood lightened as I zoomed through security and speed-walked to the gate, Brian hurrying to catch up. The Sacramento airport was crowded with arriving and departing travelers. I imagined what the arrest of an important businessman would look like in such a place. There he'd be, first or second off the plane (having enjoyed a first-class seat, of course). He'd be groggy, his expensive suit might be a little disheveled, but he would grip his briefcase and stride forward with confidence, ready to face the next challenge, order a vanilla latte, think of the next big idea, command his employees to . . .

But wait. His path is barred. He finds himself surrounded by unsmiling agents in dark suits, flashing badges, delivering news he was never expecting to hear.

Next thing he knew, he would find himself in handcuffs.

When Brian and I arrived in Dallas, I dumped my suitcase at a hotel and went straight to the Texas attorney general's headquarters. Kirsta Melton and her team were there to welcome us. I was meeting most of our Texas counterparts for the first time, though we'd been speaking on the phone for months.

We brought everyone up to speed on the arrest operation, then turned to the final step in the plan: the search of Backpage's corporate offices. Our California judge didn't have jurisdiction to issue a search warrant in a different state; Kirsta and her agents had therefore drafted one and gotten it signed by a Texas judge. Our investigation supplied most of the factual background for probable cause, and evidence seized in connection with the warrant would be shared with California.

But this is where things could get tricky, quickly. Defense attorneys routinely attempt to suppress the prosecution's evidence, as it is uniformly unfavorable to their clients. Ferrer, Larkin, and Lacey would hit us with every attack they possibly could: they would claim we lacked probable cause to search, that we gathered more documents than the warrant entitled us to, or that the evidence was stored or copied in a way that raised questions about its integrity. Our warrant and its execution needed to be airtight. I made excuses to the Texas agents about how "defendant friendly" California was to justify my insistence on perfection. We had laws like the CalECPA, which required us to notify suspects about search warrants while an investigation was still ongoing, and other laws that emphasized the rights of defendants. There was vigorous scrutiny on every decision that law enforcement makes. Further illustrating our different criminal justice climates, while I was in Texas, Kirsta got a call that a state-sanctioned execution had been carried out—something that had not happened in over a decade in California. With the common goal of a successful operation, I needed to ensure that Texas played by California rules.

Kirsta, Brian, and I discussed every aspect of the operation, carefully instructed all personnel, and went through endless contingency plans. At one point, looking at the faces of the Texas agents and lawyers, I was struck by the different worlds we lived in, not just because the police sergeants wore cowboy hats. My boss was an ambitious California Democrat, running for US Senate. Theirs was a Texas Republican. The contentious Trump-Clinton election was a month away, and the people in that room no doubt had strong opinions about what the outcome should be. But at that moment, none of it mattered. We were fighting the same fight: utterly committed to successfully bringing down Backpage.

We were ready.

Shortly after the briefing, Brian flew from Dallas to Houston with the Texas agents who would be responsible for arresting Ferrer. Much as I longed to see Ferrer's face when the agents detained him, I needed to stay in Dallas for the search of Backpage's offices, which would start as soon as Ferrer was in custody.

Meanwhile, Reye was in Arizona, searching for Lacey and Larkin. I could tell from his aggrieved texts that he felt he got the short end of the assignment stick, roaming around the desert and answering an endless stream of questions from Jessica, who was still a newbie and interested in chasing down every wild goose she could come up with. Reye was trying to do surveillance on Larkin's house, which was a hidden fortress at the end of a road. It was nearly impossible to get close enough to see anything without being seen. Multiple law enforcement agencies surveilled multiple locations because Lacey and Larkin each owned multiple homes in multiple states. Brian asked whether I wanted to wait on arresting Ferrer if we did not know where the other two were. I decided that arresting Ferrer should be the priority. I did not know if we'd have another opportunity to search the offices, and I thought that even if Lacey and Larkin fled, the case would get enough attention that it would generate some help tracking them down. "One in the hand is better than two in the bush," I told Brian. And he agreed.

Carl Ferrer's flight from the Netherlands to Houston was the longest flight of my life that I was never on. Once Homeland

Security confirmed that he had boarded United Flight 21, we tracked it on the airline's website, watching as it made its way across the world. And waiting. We couldn't raid Backpage's offices while Ferrer was in the air—inflight Wi-Fi might have notified him of our move, and he'd start destroying evidence and contacting others from whatever handheld device he had with him.

So we sat tight, making small talk and discussing the investigation ad nauseam, full of anxiety. At lunchtime, Kirsta dragged me to a legendary Texas barbeque place. The man behind the counter filled my tray with cornbread, potatoes, pulled pork, sliced tri-tip, and greens. It looked fabulous. I couldn't eat a bite. I snapped a photo and texted it to Cary, my husband, so that at least one of us could enjoy it. Then I resumed my obsessive monitoring of United.com.

At last, Flight 21 was approaching Texas. I texted Brian, needing to do something, anything, to ease my anxiety:

> **Me:** Hey, looks like his flight is landing soon?
> **Brian:** Yeah, I should probably get to the airport.

He'd been there for hours, of course, waiting like me. And I knew that this arrest would be easy compared to the arrests that officers make every day in uncontrolled street environments, with armed subjects and no backup. I should have been calm. I should have been eating barbeque! But the stakes were too high. Years of my life and countless hours of work by dozens of good people were sunk into this operation. More importantly, what we did here today would stop thousands of victims from being sold for commercial rape and would prevent thousands more from getting ensnared in Backpage's web.

Time crawled by. At last, when we knew Flight 21 was only moments from touching down, Kirsta, I, and several cars full of Texas agents parked in a lot behind Backpage's headquarters.

Finally, we got a text: Flight 21 had landed. And Brian and his team arrested Carl Ferrer without incident.

Kirsta's agents immediately stormed Backpage's shiny glass office building. I had to wait. This was standard protocol: when nonarmed personnel such as lawyers, evidence technicians, and victim advocates accompany law enforcement on an operation, the officers enter first to ensure that there are no armed or dangerous individuals at the scene. Non-law-enforcement personnel are summoned after the officers give the "all clear" signal.

I sat in the car in a daze, waiting to be summoned. It was a cloudy, gray afternoon, just starting to drizzle. Through the rain-spattered windshield, I watched the last agents rush into the building.

We got him.

I thought about Leslie and Shyla and Andrea and Genevieve and Shenevla and Lizzie and Kim and Drea and Kayla and another Kayla and all the kids who had been sold on Backpage. I thought about what this would mean to them. Lizzie had said in her interview that nobody cared about girls like her. If they cared, they wouldn't have allowed them to be sold for sex on Backpage. "How could it be illegal?" she'd asked. It was easier than ordering pizza.

I thought about Carissa Phelps, the tenacious survivor, leader, and lawyer who first talked to me about going after Backpage years ago, and how proud and gratified she would be that this day had finally come.

Then I thought, "What is taking them so long?"

As I reached for my phone, Kirsta appeared at the car window. "Come on, girlie," she said, a big smile on her face.

Before getting out of the car, I sent a text I'd been looking forward to for years.

> **Maggy:** Watch the news.
> **Yiota:** What's going on? What can you tell me?
> **Maggy:** I'll call you later. But I'm in Dallas, Texas.

Yiota, my tireless partner at the National Center for Missing & Exploited Children, knew there was only one reason for me to be in Backpage's hometown.

On my way into the building, I got a call from my press office, wanting to know if they could issue a news release. I told them to hold. Our first order of business was interviewing Ferrer's employees—if those employees saw the news before we talked with them, it could influence whether or how they answered our questions. But as it turned out, the Texas attorney general was about to start a press conference, so that got away from me.

I followed Kirsta into the tall glass building at 2501 Oak Lawn Avenue. The scene was chaotic: dozens of freaked-out employees were meandering around bullpen-style cubicles, while twenty or so Texas agents did their best to create order. As Kirsta and her team identified the employees and began the interviews, I went in search of Ferrer's office.

It was a large corner room with broad glass windows. He had a bottle of Macallan whisky on a shelf and a certificate from the FBI for "outstanding cooperation" for all the times Backpage helped law enforcement "find" victims—whom Backpage then continued to exploit and victimize.

I steeled myself and examined the place, doing a mental inventory. I was sick to my stomach, standing in this room that had served as a command center for the world's largest child-sex-trafficking operation. When agents came in for documents, I took the opportunity to escape.

After we dismissed the Backpage employees, we began identifying, seizing, and searching evidence: computers, hard drives, piles of papers, and binders of information. Following standard procedure, the officers sketched and labeled each office, listing what, if any, items would be taken. We needed to account for every piece of paper we took and precisely where we took it from. The details mattered. An incriminating document found in Ferrer's shred bin had much-greater

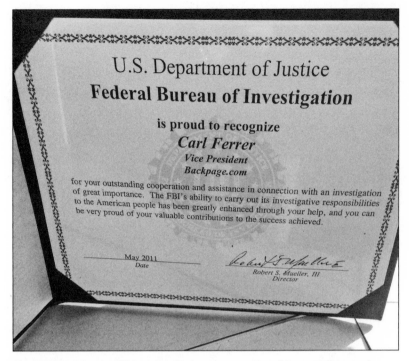

Photograph of the certificate taken during our execution of the search warrant.
(Courtesy of the author)

legal significance than one found in a low-level accountant's cubicle. Moreover, if we couldn't establish when and where we obtained an item, the court might deem it inadmissible. Despite the madness, our officers had to be organized, diligent, and totally meticulous.

The process should have been mind-numbing. In fact, it was gripping. We were looking for Backpage's policies, its financial records, and evidence that Ferrer, Larkin, and Lacey knew they were enabling sex trafficking. We were looking for communications among the three of them. And we were looking for instructions and employee manuals directing employees on how to moderate sex ads. The documents would bolster our case that Backpage was no mere internet platform but an informed, financially invested, and active enabler of sex trafficking.

The search started in the afternoon. We ordered pizza around eleven that night, careful to prop the doors open since we didn't have keys. All the agents were there, combing through files, until the following afternoon.

Larkin and Lacey were still at large. Eventually, their attorneys contacted us, and we made arrangements for them to turn themselves in, which spared them the embarrassment of a public arrest. They both showed up at the Sacramento jail and stayed in custody that weekend, pending arraignment.

At some point that evening of Ferrer's arrest, I left the Backpage offices with two Texas agents. We wanted to track down a former employee who had been deeply involved in Backpage's finances and who would have been an ideal witness for us. He wasn't home, but we decided to wait a bit. While I was in the car, I called Yiota. She told me she was getting bombarded with calls from victims, from victims' parents, and from other advocates at NCMEC. Everyone was crying with joy and overwhelmed with gratitude. An entire movement was rejoicing that Ferrer had been arrested. As sleep-deprived and brain-fogged as I was, for a few precious moments I was able to step back and relish how far we'd come. It felt unbelievably good.

Then I got a text from Brian.

> **Brian:** Can you come to Houston?
>
> **Maggy:** What? Why?
>
> **Brian:** Houston DA says Ferrer's attorneys are already at the jail trying to post bail.

Oh, no. No! I raced back to the Backpage offices and consulted with Kirsta. Everyone in Dallas seemed to think the court would let Ferrer post bail and then drag out an extradition challenge. Defendants have the right to challenge an extradition warrant, by claiming that the prosecution hasn't proved that the person they seek to extradite is the person being charged with a felony ("You got the wrong Carl Ferrer") or that the prosecution's complaint is invalid in laying out an offense.[1] None of these challenges would be successful, but they could take time for a court to sort through. This would delay our case and potentially set Ferrer on a separate track from Larkin and Lacey. The last thing we wanted was to spend months litigating extradition in Texas while Ferrer continued to jet around the world, totally unscathed by our case.

This is how millionaires gamed the justice system. With dozens of lawyers funded through Backpage, Ferrer thought he was entitled to go free—and a court was ready to listen to him.

Kirsta made a few calls, even though it was almost midnight. A friend of hers at the Houston prosecutor's office said that if I could get there in time for the 8:30 a.m. hearing and explain to the judge the significance of our case and the reasons why Ferrer was a flight risk, we might be able to keep him in custody.

It was now after midnight; our team was still searching the office, and Houston was at least a three-hour drive. It was pitch black and pouring outside. I was bleary-eyed, running on sheer adrenaline. I'd been wearing the same suit for two days, and it showed.

But I was damned if I was going to quit now.

I headed to my hotel, grabbed my bag, drove to the airport, ditched the rental car, and got myself on a 5:30 a.m. flight for Houston. Brian was waiting for me at the airport gate, as he had done for Ferrer the day before. He had spent most of the past twenty-four hours in that airport while waiting for Flight 21 and had become an expert on the food and coffee options. We got two huge cups of coffee and caught up. After the madness of the operation, all the new people and unfamiliar places, it was comforting to sit there, sipping coffee and talking, as we had so many times in Sacramento. I was trying to get my mind right for court and also make sure I hadn't missed anything while searching the offices.

"You'll never guess what Ferrer said to me when I arrested him," Brian said.

I raised my eyebrows as I took a big sip.

"He said, 'You've gotta be kidding me. After all I've done for law enforcement?' And," Brian went on, "when the agents searched his luggage? They found boxes and boxes of Viagra."

I couldn't laugh. I couldn't say anything. I just looked at Brian and drank more coffee.

At 8:00 a.m., we went to court and were ushered into chambers to meet with the district attorney and Ferrer's attorneys. Brian stayed in the hallway on his phone, trying to coordinate Lacey's surrender with the Sacramento County Sheriff's Office.

Inside, the judge sat at the head of a long table, surrounded by lawyers, all white men in dark suits. I slipped into the last seat at the table. The judge looked at me and said, "You must be the one from California," in a distinctly unimpressed, *you ain't from around here* tone of voice. He was irritated that California was generating chaos in his already-overburdened court. There were defense attorneys in fancy suits lined up outside and a host of news cameras clamoring to get inside the courtroom to get a look at the Backpage CEO.

It was clear that the judge wanted to release Ferrer on bail, making him a different court's problem. I insisted that he was a massive flight risk with unlimited liquid assets. I knew the judge would be amenable to a deal that would get Ferrer and his paparazzi out of Texas, but I had to fight hard against Ferrer's attorneys, who wanted him out of custody right away.

After some wrangling, Ferrer's attorneys agreed to waive extradition and allow us to bring him to California in custody, on one condition: he had to go that day, so he could get his bail hearing in California immediately.

Another roadblock. Brian and I had planned to send a transport team to Texas the following week to get Ferrer. Normally, the extradition process takes weeks and occurs before bail issues are addressed. We thought we'd at least have until the following week to pick him up and figured we'd need that extra time to locate the other defendants. We had all our ducks in a row, just not for *today!* But this was our one shot to bring this career criminal to the Golden State in silver handcuffs—and there was no way I was letting it slip away.

At this point, it was 9:00 a.m. in Texas, which meant it was 7:00 a.m. at home in California. My office would be deserted, and we needed logistical help to get him an airline ticket, fly him halfway across the continent, and get him booked in the Sacramento County jail.

Then Brian remembered another wrinkle: two law enforcement agents are required to transport a fugitive. We had only one— Brian. We both turned to the Texas agent who was with us. His name was Paul Hall, and he had assisted Brian with the arrest.

"Hey," I said to Paul, "I need to ask you a huge favor. Is there any way you could come to California with us? I mean today? We could even do dinner at my house?" (In my head, I was whipping up spaghetti as I pleaded for help.)

Without hesitation, Paul agreed. Then he called his wife to let her know he'd be home late—very late. This is what law enforcement is about, at its best: unwavering commitment and sacrifice; assistance offered at a moment's notice; and strong, almost familial, bonds with other officers, even ones you barely know.

There's a saying that the good people find each other—it was certainly true in this case.

I finally got my secretary on the phone and gave her all the information she needed to purchase airplane tickets for Paul Haul and Carl Ferrer. She reminded me that I needed thirty-day approval to purchase out-of-state flights. "But this is to get back to the state," I pleaded, also trying to explain the fact that although my flight was leaving from Dallas, I was actually now in Houston and needed a different flight. Eventually, I told her to just put the tickets on my personal credit card if necessary; we just needed to get it done and not get ensnared in any more bureaucracy. I never imagined I'd be offering to buy Carl Ferrer a ticket to California, but here we were.

At last, we filed into the courtroom to watch the judge formally call the case and for Ferrer to waive extradition on the record.

Brian lingered in the back while I went up front, taking a seat right behind the Houston prosecutors. Ferrer's attorneys were crowded together at defense counsel's table.

The judge entered. Several bailiffs ushered in a group of criminal defendants whose cases were being processed that morning.

That's when I saw Ferrer in person for the first time.

I'd been seeing his photo for years. I'd even watched video from some tech convention, where a thousand people heard him speak. There he wore expensive, well-tailored clothes, a tidy goatee, and stylish glasses. He was tanned and well groomed, bursting with confidence and privilege. His face was up on a big screen, and he was talking about the next generation of internet advertising and how it would change the world. The audience was listening to him. They admired him as an entrepreneur. He had clout. He had power.

But in that Houston courtroom, he wore a baggy orange jumpsuit. His hands and feet were shackled. He looked exhausted and pale, crumpled, his sandy hair disheveled. He stood, clearly miserable, among a group of men who were being charged with committing heinous crimes that inflicted immeasurable pain on other people.

In other words, Carl Ferrer was exactly where he belonged.

I doubt he ever thought he'd be surrounded by those sorts of people, wearing the same cheap uniform. I doubt he ever thought his day of reckoning with the criminal justice system would come. But it had, and in that moment, Backpage's millions of dollars couldn't help him.

The judge began addressing Ferrer. I listened, soaking in what was happening. Here we were: the culmination of years of work, all-nighters, and untold stress. I turned and caught Brian's eye. We exchanged a look that encompassed all of that:

We got him.

Later that day, Brian, the Texas agent, and Ferrer departed on one flight, and I flew back on another, exhausted, relieved, and grateful. I slept for the first time in days.

Carl Ferrer in custody in Texas court. (Courtesy of the author)

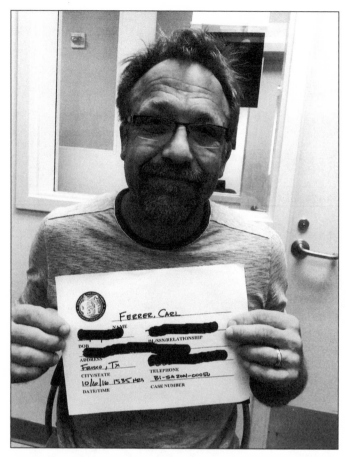

Carl Ferrer's arrest shot. (Courtesy of the author)

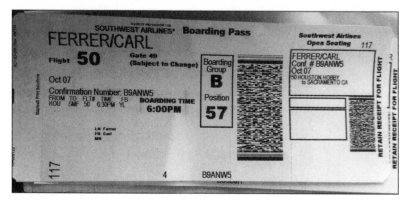

Carl Ferrer's boarding pass. (Courtesy of the author)

8

ROUND 1

CARL Ferrer arrived in California amid a media frenzy. The very first court appearance was on a Tuesday afternoon in October 2016. The day before had been a court holiday, so the three defendants had been in jail over the weekend without having seen a California judge yet. Larkin and Lacey had traveled to Sacramento on their own rather than being hunted down. They turned themselves in to the Sacramento County jail late Friday and were safely in custody by the time I got off the plane from Texas. We knew these defendants would be well represented, but we were not sure who the California defense team would be. Larkin and Lacey had attempted to post bail over the weekend but were unable to do so because of a source-of-funds bail motion we had filed. This essentially meant that the defendants would have to show and the judge would have to find that the money they were posting for bail was not obtained feloniously. With their investments and connections, we knew they would be able to accomplish this at some point; but we wanted the court to ensure that the money paying their bail was clean money, and this additional hoop kept them in jail over a three-day weekend.

As much as these defendants demanded special treatment, our goal was for their case to be treated like any other felony case that came in the door. On any given Tuesday afternoon in Department 60 and in arraignment courts across the country, in-custody defendants are read charges against them, appointed counsel, and then allowed to address bail. Many defendants charged with much less serious crimes spend much longer than a weekend behind bars, yet we knew they would be outraged by the arrests and try to completely flip the narrative.

Instead of preparing for court, I had spent that morning in synagogue. It was Yom Kippur, the Jewish Day of Atonement and the holiest day of the year. If you are only going to go to one religious service in an entire year as a Jew, it is supposed to be this one, despite the outsized attention that Hanukkah commands in the holiday card aisle. Yom Kippur is a chance to reflect and repent for wrongdoing during the prior year and to forgive others who may have wronged you—a self-check-in. My connection with God gives me faith, strength, and hope. I needed that fortitude for my day job. I managed to slip out of services a few minutes early, though, still praying for forgiveness as I sped downtown to the Attorney General's Office.

I grabbed my Backpage binder and my new co-counsel, Randy Mailman, for the eight-block walk down I Street to the jail courthouse where they would be arraigned. Randy and I had worked well together on a major fraud case, in which defense shenanigans made me appreciate her matter-of-fact demeanor, dramatic sense of humor, and well-planned punches. She had a way with words and would invent clever one-liners that deftly summed up our cases, often crediting her mother. We had strategized the Backpage bail issues while I was in Texas, and we were excited to be working together again. She had recently transferred from the LA office and was eager to get to work on this massive case and take on new challenges. Randy had a great style about her—she was always impeccably dressed in whatever was trending at J. Crew. She was witty, clear-headed, and decisive. It was all especially impressive knowing that she had a baby boy at home and was already pregnant with another. We both wore flipflops with our suits around the office but kept shelves of colorful heels behind our desks. It was fun having someone to pick out shoes with before court!

When we got to court for our first Backpage appearance in California, a flurry of people were already crowded around the entrance to the courthouse and filling the hallways. Most of the people were survivors and victim advocates there to support the prosecution. A group called Shared Hope had organized volunteers, who wore red and attended each court hearing in solidarity with trafficking victims. When they noticed the red pumps I had picked from my office shoe collection, they took it as a sign. Their support was incredibly meaningful throughout the proceedings—no matter what was happening in court, the advocates reminded me at every moment whom I was there for.

But outside the courthouse, there was also a vocal group of women protesting the prosecution. They were sex workers, calling out law enforcement for disrupting Backpage and criminalizing rather than legalizing prostitution. I wasn't there to invalidate their experiences, but the case was about exploitation—about child victims and those who never exercised free will. I didn't begrudge the sex workers their right to express their opinions, but the evidence showed that Backpage was facilitating the trafficking of thousands of vulnerable victims as young as twelve.

In a sense, the sex workers merely emphasized our point that Backpage was an online brothel. The fact that some transactions were not commercial rape did not weaken our prosecution. I had only had protestors on one other case—it was with Dave in San Francisco. We were prosecuting the murder of Sergeant John Young, a police officer who was assassinated in his prime by a terrorist group called the Black Liberation Army in 1971. The radical group made it their mission to ambush and murder police throughout the country. Dave had resurrected a cold case, attempting to finally bring justice to the aggrieved police department and to Sergeant Young's widow. But decades later, we walked into a San Francisco courthouse only to find people clamoring to stand with the defendants in solidarity. "You go first," Dave joked to me as we weaved through a shouting mob just to get to counsel table. Dave was respectful toward protestors and remained focused on the facts and the law. I would follow his example.

That first hearing lasted less than five minutes. The court was not prepared for the chaos and media circus, had a busy felony calendar, and seemed unsure exactly what to do with all of the many defense attorneys who had shown up to represent the Backpage trio. The judge, Michael Bowman, read the name of each defendant, Carl Ferrer, James Larkin, and Michael Lacey. They stood together behind metal bars that separate the in-custody defendant area from the rest of the courtroom. I could still remember looking at the faces of the young, exploited women I saw in a Stockton courtroom standing behind similar bars more than ten years before, numb, lifeless, and empty as they blankly stared into space without expectation. Ferrer, Lacey, and Larkin stared back.

Each was clad in an orange jumpsuit labeled "Sac County Prisoner." The media snapped pictures, and the many onlookers strained to get a glimpse of these three once-prominent businessmen locked in a cage. The defendants were furious that they were still in jail and that they had remained there over a holiday weekend. Moreover, they wouldn't be getting released immediately, because there was nothing the defense could do prior to the bail hearing, which neither the court nor the defense was prepared for that day. After a long list of defense attorneys introduced themselves and recorded their names as counsel for one or more of the defendants, Judge Bowman set the case for further proceedings and a bail hearing. Judge Bowman was relatively new. I hadn't appeared in front of him before, but he had a good reputation. His experience as a lawyer had been in private practice, when he handled both civil cases and criminal defense. Optimistically, I thought that was a good thing. He would be able to call BS on the defendants and would be familiar with criminal procedure.

After court adjourned, Randy and I walked up to the gaggle of defense attorneys to introduce ourselves and provide our contact information. It is customary for the defense and prosecution to exchange pleasantries, work together to calendar hearings, and freely discuss various aspects of the case. Even though it is an adversarial system, there are many junctures throughout litigation where there are opportunities to find common ground.

Defendants in custody at arraignment in Sacramento County Superior Court
(Courtesy of the *Sacramento Bee*)

Two of the defense lawyers were partners at well-known Bay Area criminal defense firms with solid reputations. Others in the group were longtime Backpage defenders from Arizona, who would be appearing *pro hac vice* (Latin for visiting from another court with permission) for this case. There was the father-daughter Henze team—Janie Henze and her dad, Tom Henze—who were polite and cheerful and welcomed our Sacramento restaurant recommendations. There was also David Dratman, a strident local attorney whom Randy was in the midst of clashing with on another case. It wasn't clear what his role on the defense team would be, perhaps merely to provide insight on the court and our office as local counsel.

And then there was Jim Grant, who seemed to be the self-appointed leader of the bunch. He was a partner at a big law firm in Seattle and a dedicated Backpage defender. He had successfully shot down lawsuits against Backpage in the past and gone on the offensive against anyone who sought to question internet rights in any way. He sauntered over to me as I was collecting my papers and confidently introduced himself. "I am Jim Grant, partner with Davis, Tremaine & Wright. I am the First Amendment lawyer.

First Amendment. Did you do any constitutional research before filing this case?" There were many ways to respond. "Nice to meet you, Mr. Grant," I said politely.

Randy and I headed down I Street and back to the office. "Nothing bad happened," we reported to our anxious colleagues. Next up was prepping for the bail hearing. At the bail hearing, the defense would produce evidence, either through documents or live witnesses, showing that the funds they were using to post bail came from a source other than their criminal operation.

In the ensuing days, though, before we even got to bail, the defense team filed hundreds of pages of motions to dismiss. They argued that the Communications Decency Act mandated that the case be dismissed immediately and that it never should have been filed. They claimed the CDA was a flat-out bar to any prosecution as opposed to a defense to bring up later in the proceedings. I knew that this would be their strategy—I even saw emails back and forth in which the defendants asked an employee to make edits to the Wikipedia page's definition of Communications Decency Act! This would ensure that reporters and the general public would see things from their vantage point before we got a chance to make our case. They reached out to editorial boards around the country pushing for articles to be published about how dangerous this case would be for online speech.

They also wasted no time in painting a narrative of political opportunism—Attorney General Harris was locked in a political battle for a US Senate seat, and the case, which garnered nationwide media attention, had been filed mere weeks before the election. "Harris just wanted to put our clients on a perp walk to bolster her political career," they claimed. Of course, this meant nothing to me and the law enforcement team that actually worked the case—I would have much rather filed it years before! But we couldn't file it until it was ready, until we had approval, until we had signed warrants, until we had law enforcement help in Texas, and so on. It was a long, complicated, multistep process.

Newspaper editorials bantered about how our case muzzled free speech, and powerful internet interest groups suddenly sprouted up as "watchdogs" of government abuse. They never bothered to consider the charges: conspiracy and *receiving* commercial sex proceeds from sexually exploited minors. In my mind, we were prosecuting the defendants for *conduct*, not speech. Moreover, the site was still selling children for sex—how could these advertisements for illegal activity be considered protected speech? But I felt the weight of going against the legal grain. Jim Grant sent our office a letter requesting to meet with the attorney general directly, implying that we were incompetent or rogue prosecutors who hadn't properly understood or explained the case. "This case should be dismissed immediately," he said, and a bevy of "First Amendment lawyers" repeated it. Larkin and Lacey were even directly quoted in articles attacking the case.

In my career, I had never encountered such arrogance and entitlement. I prosecuted real-estate brokers who knew it all and thought they'd never get caught; I prosecuted sex traffickers who assumed their victims would never tell on them; I even prosecuted a murderer who, after being convicted of first-degree murder, muttered at me, "I'll be out in two years, bitch." But I never had defendants call my boss and demand that a case be dismissed and seriously believe that they were entitled to skip the entire criminal justice system because they had a constitutional challenge.

Illegal searches, illegal arrests, illegal confessions—those are all constitutional challenges and the bread and butter of defense work. The prosecution must prove that each piece of evidence is obtained lawfully, that each arrest lies on probable cause, that each defendant statement is voluntarily given and only following the reading of Miranda rights. And rightly so.

Defense attorneys are a critical check on the prosecution's power and serve the vital function of representing indigent defendants against the power of government. We welcomed the challenge of proving our case and looked forward to showing why our prosecution was constitutionally valid. Yet the defense team was arguing in its early motions that the prosecution should not even get a hearing to prove what the defendants did and how they did it. Their mere assertion that all charged crimes involved the website gave them a sweeping cloak of immunity that they claimed could never be pierced.

We knew that we had to make the point that the defendants were charged with committing crimes and that the evidence needed to be examined at the preliminary hearing, like any other criminal case. The defense's strategy was to treat it as a civil case. Multiple civil cases had already been dismissed against Backpage and other websites, and they wanted to be able to rely on those cases as precedent. We needed to counter that the Communications Decency Act could not be used to shield them from criminal liability for pimping or any other felony offenses that were consistent with federal law. Sure, the CDA protected from frivolous lawsuits against internet service providers based on third-party speech and conduct, but it should never be a shield for criminal liability and especially not for sex trafficking, when we could show that they actively participated in content creation. Moreover, because we would be showing that the defendants acted with criminal intent, they should not be entitled to First Amendment protection. We were prosecuting them for knowingly receiving money from sex trafficking—how could that possibly be a valid exercise of free speech?

But before we got to that, we had the bail hearing. Of course, they were eager to get out of jail when they learned the case would not be dismissed immediately. As we knew would happen, the defense brought evidence to show that the defendants had access to ample amounts of money outside of the Backpage business. But the actual source of funds was still murky and was being vouched for by Don Bennett Moon, another Backpage shareholder whom we recognized from the information provided by the National Center for Missing & Exploited Children, the notes that Yiota had provided me from the meetings of the former NCMEC CEO Ernie Allen with Mike Lacey, James Larkin, and Don Moon. At those meetings, the executives were crude and unapologetically committed to the proliferation of Backpage, and displayed a callous disregard for the devastating suffering of sex-trafficking victims. Since Moon was posting the bail, on our request, Judge Bowman called him to testify so that he could explain that the bail funds were from a legitimate source.

Even though Moon was quite wealthy, he looked sort of scruffy, with messy facial hair and an oversized coat. As he answered questions, he seemed bothered by the whole ordeal, as if the justice system was beneath him and his money should get him whatever he wanted—whether it be a teenage girl or his friends out of jail.

We had discussed charging him as a codefendant but ultimately determined we did not have enough evidence, at least not yet. He was a lawyer, which meant we couldn't review his emails, at least not without involving a special master and having the content reviewed for attorney-client privilege. A special master is a person appointed by the court to take custody of evidence over which a privilege is claimed. This is the accepted process for reviewing emails to or from attorneys to ensure that the attorney-client privilege is not breached. When people communicate with their lawyer to seek legal advice, those communications are confidential, unless they are in furtherance of the commission of a crime, a call for a judge or special master to make. We knew Moon was deeply involved and a major beneficiary of the company; yet we did not feel we could charge him without more direct evidence, and we didn't have the bandwidth to take on the added layer of complexity that searching his communications would entail. But here he was in Department 60, sitting on the witness stand, in a closed court hearing, discussing his money that was supposedly unrelated to Backpage.

Randy took the lead on questioning him. She was well prepared and seemed excited for the courtroom showdown with one of

Backpage's slimiest backers. But every other question she posed, the defense objected, and the judge was sustaining the objections. "This is a bail hearing, counsel, stay within the scope," Judge Bowman barked after several sustained objections. But Randy had a plan, and the questions did relate to bail, even if the court couldn't connect the dots yet. Randy was setting up a chess move, but the Court didn't have the patience to allow it to unfold.

Randy explained the relevance of her questions in the hopes that the Court would see where she was going, but instead, as a former defense attorney, he suddenly seemed offended.

"Are you saying, counsel, that an attorney who receives funds from a client needs to show where the money came from? That's privileged."

Randy countered, "Not necessarily, your honor—if an attorney is knowingly accepting the proceeds of crime, there is a crime-fraud exception which pierces the attorney-client privilege. The attorney can be a coconspirator or be part of a money laundering . . ."

But before she could finish, the defense attorneys interrupted. "Judge, your analysis is correct. The prosecutor is clearly fishing, coming up with all these crazy scenarios that have nothing to do with this case. This gentleman has had to travel all the way here, taken the stand, and been made to answer sensitive questions about his financial wealth. Now the prosecutor wants to have a trial on unrelated tangents? This needs to stop."

Randy was fuming, but I could tell that the judge agreed with the defense.

Even though I disagreed, and believed we should have been allowed to fully examine the source of the funds, I didn't want to use all our firepower on a bail hearing. We expected the defendants to be out of custody anyway. There was no amount of bail that they wouldn't be able to come up with, and after their faces were plastered all over the news, I was less worried that they would successfully be able to disappear. Our credibility with the judge was far more important than whether his analysis was erroneous or how quickly they were released. We needed to gain the court's trust—he needed to see us as reasonable, credible, even-keeled, even if we were throwing a fit on the inside.

I backed us up out of the questioning and thanked the Court for ensuring that the posted bail was not obtained feloniously. Judge Bowman nodded. "I understand the prosecution is doing its job here, and I appreciate the thorough bail examination, counsel." He agreed with my suggestions that the defendants be ordered to remain in the United States with surrendered passports, apprise counsel of any travel plans, and make all court appearances, unless their presence was explicitly waived.

In my mind, we walked out of that first hearing relatively unscathed and had also picked up some new facts about how the defendants were operating and obtaining their money. In Randy's mind, this was an ominous sign of rulings to come.

"So much for treating the defendants like regular criminal defendants," Randy snapped. "It will be fine. It's just the bail hearing," I said optimistically. "And Randy, you were on fire in there," I added, sensing that her hurt ego was making the problem worse.

"Ugh, what a disaster," Randy retorted.

The next time we were in court, Judge Bowman set a schedule for briefing on the motions to dismiss. The defense would be filing all of their objections to our charges, we would have a few days to respond, and then they would reply. After slogging through a few more court appearances where the defense objected to bail conditions (they weren't allowed to leave the country), subpoenas we were serving on third parties (they wanted our investigation to cease immediately), and seeking additional time to file more motions (our response to their motion was so egregious that they needed more time), the court finally set a date for final arguments on the merits of the dismissal motion. We were still in Department 60, the courtroom attached to the jail, but the defendants were now appearing out of custody. It was a day I was looking forward to. I was confident we would prevail, and I was eager to move the case forward to the next phase of litigation—a preliminary hearing and then a trial.

But on the morning of that court appearance, Judge Bowman issued an unexpected tentative written ruling dismissing the case. A tentative ruling tells the parties which way the judge is leaning. It is not a final decision, as arguments can still be considered, but it is an indication of the court's thinking at that time. It was unusual for a judge on a criminal case to issue a written tentative ruling at this phase of the proceedings, especially before arguments had even occurred. Tentative rulings are typically issued in civil cases either to narrow the arguments or to encourage the parties to settle. Why on earth was it happening in our case? And why on earth was he leaning toward dismissing the entire thing? I waved goodbye as our strategy of "treat this case like every other criminal case" was rapidly free-falling off a cliff.

Before I actually had a chance to read the ruling, the chief deputy attorney general was calling, asking me what had gone wrong and how I was going to fix it. I had made a quick run to Big 5 to get a mouth guard for my son, who had a football game later that day, and was still trying to get the opinion from the clerk so that I could read it and answer those questions. Of course, the defense team had their press people and the media all queued up with stories about how badly we had bungled the case. The breaking news was that the case had already been dismissed, even though the ruling was supposedly tentative. Everyone was freaking out, and I was trying to hold it together.

As I tried to read the ruling and think through how to counter it, my phone did not stop buzzing with concern and frustration. The press office and the attorney general were calling, the media was asking for the attorney general's statement on the dismissal ruling, victim advocates and colleagues were panicking, and I had to be in court in less than an hour.

As a prosecutor, I had to tune out the media and argue my case in court. Prosecutors also must abide by professional rules of conduct that largely prevent us from disclosing factual information about pending cases. Since defendants are presumed innocent until proven guilty, saying anything to the media that could be construed as undermining that presumption could potentially be challenged in court as a violation of the defendant's due process rights.

But defense attorneys tend to speak when they feel it is in the best interest of their client, and when they have millions of dollars, the media is one more of their tools. I walked through a chaotic sea of people into the courtroom and up to counsel table. I couldn't talk to anyone. I was too mad at myself. Even though I had reviewed the complaint dozens of times, I hadn't thought it through enough in the context of a CDA dismissal motion because I wrongly assumed that I would be allowed to put on evidence showing that the defendants were outside of the CDA's protection. I thought that making allegations about the CDA on the complaint would somehow signal the court to treat the case differently from other criminal cases, where complaints are relatively barebones and the only real requirement is that the defendant have notice of the charge. But if I had elaborately alleged that the CDA did not apply on the face of the complaint, rather than assume that it didn't, I would not be in a defensive posture without factual allegations on the record.

Yiota had flown in from DC for the court hearing. It was our first time meeting in person, even though she had been with me every step of the way. Of course, I had envisioned that we would be together celebrating advancing the case to the next step, not wallowing in an untimely dismissal ruling. I knew the case would be challenging, but I expected at least a chance to put on the evidence.

I wanted a preliminary hearing so I could put the defendants on trial. When the judge saw those victims and what the defendants were doing, how could he possibly give them a pass? Most frustrating was that I had evidence that the defendants helped create content for the website. This meant that they were not simply a platform protected by the CDA but an actor outside the scope of the CDA's protection. But in order to show this, I needed to present the case—witnesses and documents and emails. I explained all of this to the court—that, if given the opportunity, I could show that Ferrer affirmatively bought other websites out of the market, that he created ads for his other sites, that he coached traffickers on how to post ads without alerting law enforcement.

I argued that the Communications Decency Act is not an absolute bar to any criminal prosecution involving a website and by its own terms does not apply to the enforcement of state criminal law that is consistent with federal law.

> The CDA specifically exempts the enforcement of federal criminal law from its purview including any state law that is consistent. Indeed, it would be ludicrous to expect that a defendant who designed and profited from a website wholly dedicated to an illegal and dangerous purpose would not be subject to prosecution just because a website was his or her means of carrying out the crime. A defendant could create a site exclusively for selling narcotics, or stolen property, or soliciting murder for that matter. Prosecuting these sorts of crimes is not inconsistent with federal law, but instrumental to the State's police powers.
>
> The criminal culpability of such a defendant rests on multiple factors such as his or her knowledge and intent, whether the defendant was merely a neutral publisher or affirmatively contributed to the illegal conduct, and whether the defendant created some or all of the content that aided in carrying out the crime. The People maintain that a preliminary hearing, and not a dismissal motion, is the appropriate avenue to establish such facts and show why these Defendants are not entitled to CDA defense. However, based on the court's tentative ruling the People will preview some of the evidence that we intend to present at the preliminary hearing.[1]

I told the court about how the Defendants created two websites called EvilEmpire and Big City and that the defendants specifically selected and manipulated photos and data from Backpage escort ads in order to create new profiles for victims on these alternative sites. The victims themselves could neither post these ads nor take them down. Only the defendants had control over them. I argued,

> The evidence will show that the victims listed in counts 2 through 6 and 9 through 10 were all direct victims of this manipulative and deceitful practice and that none of the victims were aware that Defendants were manipulating their photographs and information to create Defendants' EvilEmpire and Big City websites. Defendants developed these sites to further their illegal purposes by both eliminating competition and deceiving companies that would not do business with Backpage because of the illegal nature of their ads.
>
> Defendants' actions in exploiting the victims' likeness and information not only constituted the creation and development of content, but also violated the victims' rights of publicity. Intellectual property violations, which include violations of the right to publicity, are expressly and separately outside the scope of the CDA. Those very violations were also the means, in part, by which Defendants committed the conspiracy and perpetrated the other charged crimes. Aside and separate from Defendants' actions in developing content, the People reiterate that the CDA does not immunize Defendants from state criminal prosecution and disagree with the Court's characterization of Defendants as publishers. The People seek to hold Defendants responsible for *their own misconduct*, not for others' speech. This is not a case against Backpage, a website; it is a case against three individual defendants who used multiple platforms to commercially sexually exploit vulnerable women and children. That is the core of the People's prosecution; and nothing in the CDA was intended to preclude the People from proving that case.[2]

Judge Bowman set a timeline for the parties to file additional briefing and said he would take the case under submission—in other words, he would decide later whether to finalize his tentative ruling or change course.

After court, I went to the Torch Club with Yiota. It was a dingy, dark bar that had great live blues music at night. But in the afternoon, the Torch was dependably empty. When I walked in, the bartender sympathetically handed me an ice-cold Bud Light and a bowl of Chex Mix as if he already knew I had had a bad day. He probably got an alert about the case being dismissed! Yiota was a great sport about the whole thing. She wasn't bothered that she had sandwiched a terribly disappointing court ruling between two red-eye flights within a twenty-four-hour period. Even though everything had gone wrong, she was hopeful that it would be all right. She thought the hearing went well. "You pulled this off the rails, gave the judge a lot to think about," she reassured me. Even the media was walking back its dismissal headlines, instead summarizing the prosecution's arguments and reporting that the court took the matter under submission. It wasn't *over* over.

Back at my office, the team was upbeat. Jackie Salvi, our team's trusted paralegal, would reassure me that the case wasn't getting dismissed. When I interviewed Jackie for the job, I learned that she had started her career, like me, in Stockton. She had been a paralegal at the District Attorney's Office and was looking for the next step in her career. After working with her for about a month, I suggested she take the LSAT and told her she was as good as any lawyer! She rejected my advice, but I had the benefit of working with her on most of my cases. She was no-nonsense, tough, and direct but also hilarious and kind. When I would wallow about Backpage and stress about how court had gone, she would insist that I snap out of it. "Lock it up," she would say. I often blamed myself, saying how badly I felt about this or that. "Stop with all the feels," she would say. She was funny and helpful and knew me as well an anyone.

At least once a week, I would have lunch with Reye in the office cafeteria. We both would always get BLTs, enjoying the reliably crispy bacon and the chance to catch up. We discussed all of our cases, ideas for new cases, and what I would do with my life if Backpage was over. I couldn't even imagine.

But about a month after that argument, on December 9, 2016, the written ruling dismissing the case was finalized. In the conclusion of the ruling, Judge Bowman stated, "The Court understands the importance and urgency in waging war against sexual exploitation"; however, he concluded that the Communications Decency Act was a "complete shield" from liability for websites like Backpage. "Congress has spoken on this matter, and it is for Congress, not the Court, to revisit."[3]

I was devastated. It was the kind of knockout blow that makes you wonder whether you can ever get up again. And I didn't understand the logic behind the well-written, carefully worded conclusion that completely gutted my case.

Maybe we were just ahead of our time. In 2017, the US Senate would issue a scathing report detailing how Backpage was trafficking children.[4] The Senate would then refer the matter to the United States attorney general for criminal charges. A year later, the #MeToo movement would rock the world—from Hollywood to the Capitol, widespread sexual harassment and abuse would be exposed and society's tolerance for it would finally be called into question. And then in 2019, Jeffrey Epstein, the powerful financier and personal friend of President Donald Trump, would be indicted for sex trafficking, and everyone would finally talk about how horrific—and prevalent—it is. But here we were, stuck in the gloom of 2016, when everyone seemed content to look the other way. "This isn't my problem" was what the court ruling seemed to say.

I missed Dave. I wanted to send him the ruling. He would have hated it as much as I did, but he would have found some silver lining or at least made me laugh. At some point, I had helped Dave load the emoji keyboard onto his phone—he started adding smiley faces and winks to nearly every message he sent me. Then he discovered monkeys, ghosts, and tacos. I am sure if he were alive, he would have filled my screen with the poop emoji and then explained that the ruling cuts both ways. I tried to channel his positive energy.

I had a regular staff meeting with my team—the kind where each person gives an update on their cases. My big case was the elephant in the room, but I wasn't having a pity party. The other attorneys methodically talked though their cases—what they were filing, what they were offering to settle, what help they needed, and what the defense was arguing. We went into the weeds on issues like charging decisions, whether to charge securities fraud or grand theft, whether to seek enhancements, and the provability of financial loss. We discussed overarching questions—like the goal of the prosecution and whether the defendant needed to go to prison for his or her crime. As usual, I chimed in with follow-up questions, prodding at arguments I thought were weak and pushing my staff to consider all theories.

Finally, I owned the dismissal of the Backpage charges:

> I filed the case against Backpage because I believed in it. I truly thought the outcome would be different. Others questioned whether this case would be able to proceed and whether it was worth the risk, and perhaps the judge has proved them right in dismissing the case. To the extent that this reflects poorly on our office and our team, I apologize. But I still believe in this case and have no regret about charging it. As your supervisor, what I want from you more than anything is to be fearless in seeking justice. Be smart, be thorough, be open-minded, be careful, but never be afraid to do what is right.

9

WINTER

I SPENT the two weeks after the case dismissal in dismal silence at work. In addition to being devastated about the case, the Niners were experiencing a historically bad season. Meanwhile, Harris had won her race for the US Senate. Her executive team had mostly gone with her to DC or were starting new jobs at big law firms, and my team was already thinning out for the holidays. Other than stress-eating my way through Tyler's chocolate Advent calendar, I hadn't done much to prepare for the holidays. Instead, I was feverishly pursuing a new angle: drafting money-laundering charges against Ferrer, Larkin, and Lacey—$45 million worth, to be exact.

There were many points during the investigation when I had considered money-laundering charges. They would be provable without victim testimony and less likely to be dismissed on Communications Decency Act grounds. Rather than focusing on the website itself and the defendants' advertising, we would be focusing on their sources of money and how they conducted their illicit business. But to successfully prosecute money-laundering charges, we needed evidence from the defendants' banking institutions.

During the investigation, we were afraid that making contact with the banks could give the defendants a heads-up that they were being investigated. We couldn't afford that. We thought it would result in us getting sued by Backpage, in an attempt to shut us down before we were able to even file our case. They had been successful with this aggressive strategy in the past, including against the Cook County sheriff of Chicago. In that case, the sheriff sent a letter warning major banks that by doing business with Backpage, they were enabling human trafficking. In response,

Backpage sued the sheriff, claiming that his letter had a chilling effect on free speech and citing Backpage's rights under the CDA. We did not want to be in court with Backpage until we had criminal charges, backed up by solid evidence. So, simultaneous with the arrest of the defendants and search of Backpage headquarters back in October, we served search warrants on major banks that Backpage had done business with. Now, this new financial evidence was finally available for review.

A prosecutor's ethical obligation is to only file charges when she has a good-faith belief she can prove those charges beyond a reasonable doubt. Without records from the banks, we were close but not quite there. You can't just charge a defendant with extra crimes that you think he may have committed or rely on the fact that he committed other terrible crimes to bootstrap additional charges. You need to make sure that each charge, on its own, will hold up for each defendant. So there I was a couple of weeks before Christmas, searching through newly obtained evidence from our October search warrants to determine whether we had enough to prove money laundering.

I was in frequent contact with Bassem Banafa, a forensic auditor whom I had first met when he was working in the insurance fraud unit of the Contra Costa County District Attorney's Office. In a roundabout way, while investigating worker's compensation insurance fraud, Bassem had discovered a network of over one hundred massage-parlor brothels and was looking for assistance building and prosecuting a major case, similar to what Reye and I had done with Operation Wilted Flower. Bassem and I immediately clicked—I could tell that he had poured hours and hours of his life into putting together the pieces to make a successful large-scale conspiracy and money-laundering case, and yet no one at his office seemed to be listening to him.

Bassem was mildly friendly, severely quirky, and smart beyond any human I'd ever encountered. He worked like a mad scientist—often in his own world but committed to connecting his work to improving our world. If I could only filter his smartness into translatable and usable information, the sky was the limit. I had worked out an agreement with his district attorney in which I would assist on the massage-parlor cases and Bassem would assist us on Backpage. And now, armed with fresh financial data we received from the October search warrants and in a severe time crunch, he was the perfect wizard to turn to.

Bassem was culling the new data for evidence corroborating our money-laundering theory. We needed to be sure that each dollar was accounted for—that each transaction initiated on the website advertising a girl in a California city went to the corresponding Backpage bank account and then to various Backpage expenses, including to the defendants. The exact amount of each money transaction mattered. The method of payment mattered. Many of the payments at this point were cryptocurrency, like Bitcoin, and to simplify our case, we were focusing on specific commercial banks and filtering out cryptocurrency. Certain types of payments went through so many processors that they became impossible to trace. This was money laundering at its most successful.

Bassem sorted an enormous swath of data in multiple ways to make it usable. He stayed up late into the night, and I wouldn't hear from him during regular business hours. But then he would suddenly emerge with spreadsheets, reports, and referenced page numbers from our evidence database.

I spent most of my time in my office with the door closed. I was structuring the charges, checking Bassem's data, researching the next phase of defense dismissal motions, which I knew were inevitable, and reading every case on money laundering I could find. But there wasn't a case like mine. I would again be in uncharted legal territory.

The weather outside was stormy. Gusts of wind were flinging rain pellets at my office window. It looked like it could be nighttime all day long, and technically, it was the shortest days of the year. Fueled by peanut-butter pretzels and making my way through a sixer of Diet Coke, I spent hours and hours uninterrupted in my Backpage cave drafting a new complaint based on a new theory supported by new evidence. I was bunkered down, in the dead of winter, preparing for war.

I finally emerged with a draft complaint two days before Christmas. I excitedly ran down the hall to Randy's office with a hard copy in hand. I was delighted to find that she was still there, but I could tell by her reaction that she was not ready to deal with Backpage 2.0. She had hoped we would regroup in the new year and thoughtfully discuss the case and potential options with the new administration after the holidays. She didn't really know the extent of what I had been through to get the case filed in the first place—that I'd spent months and months and written memos and memos just to get the case out the door. She wasn't nearly as attached to the case (which was probably a good thing overall), so the idea that it may not get approved again probably didn't tear her heart out the way it did mine.

But emotions aside, I was holding a solid complaint with well-thought-out charges based on specific and credible evidence. The standard for every prosecutor on every case is the same—you must have a good-faith belief you can prove the charges. I had that belief, and to me, holding the complaint back while sex-trafficking victims continued to be tortured through Backpage was unconscionable.

I left Randy with the complaint. I told her to read it through for me and let me know what she thought. I was her supervisor and did not need her permission, but I valued her input and wanted her on board. I wanted us to be making this major decision together. And I certainly didn't want her to be uncomfortable with the way we were proceeding.

I popped back into her office about forty minutes later. She wanted more time—weeks or possibly months. The money-laundering charges weren't straightforward, she was nervous about bringing back the pimping charges, and she didn't like being rushed into a huge decision on the highest-stakes case of her career. Everything she said made sense. Her stubbornness was something I liked about her. She was decisive and dead to right about her opinions. I valued that certainty, even if it meant that I sometimes had to field calls from angry defense attorneys saying she wouldn't budge on an offer or frustrated cops saying she wouldn't agree to file a case unless she got her way on some detail. She was steadfast and consistent with an unwavering commitment to what she believed to be right.

But there I was, standing at her office door, anxious to sign the complaint and take it to court before close of business but barricaded between her stubbornness and my uneasiness in acting without her agreement. The complaint automatically has the name of the attorney general on it. Underneath that name, there would normally be the name of a supervisor or other attorney who reviewed the filing and, underneath that, the attorney filing the case, who would actually sign the complaint.

And so I broke the silence by offering to take her name off the complaint. "You'll still be cocounsel on this case, if you want to be. And I can add your name to a later filing. We'll probably have to file an amended version of this complaint anyway. But I am filing this complaint now. Do you want your name on it?" She thought about it for a few more minutes before saying, "I trust you. If your name is on it, my name is on it."

That was that. I printed out the complaint, signed it, made six copies for the court clerk, and walked through rain and wind on a stormy Friday afternoon, two days before Christmas. The ink was a little smudged, and the first copy was dotted with rain drops; but I knew the charges would stand. They had to. The clerk filestamped my complaint, handed back my stamped copies, and entered the new charges into the system. We exchanged merry Christmas wishes, and I walked out of the courthouse and back into the blistering wind. Everyone was gone when I got back to the office.

I clutched my wet complaint copy in silent satisfaction. This was it. I knew that it was Friday night of Christmas weekend, but I texted Yiota anyway. She was thrilled that we were giving it another shot and eager to see how the money-laundering challenges would turn out.

While I still believed in the pimping charges because the defendants were plainly violating the pimping statute through their own actions, regardless of being publishers, the money-laundering charges were even stronger from a CDA perspective. There was no way the CDA could protect them from what was solely their actions and not those of a third party. I knew we would be attacked. I expected the defense to kick and scream, possibly even demand sanctions or try and take my bar card. I knew that they would use their money, their power, and every tool at their disposal to dismantle me and my case. And I didn't care.

While I scurried around the mall scrambling to buy gifts for my kids and nephews and nieces and in-laws, I thought about the other kids—the kids in my complaint, the kids whom NCMEC still hadn't located, the kids who would spend Christmas in jail or in a motel room. Even on Christmas, Backpage was running thousands of ads.

One of those ads was for a sixteen-year-old girl named Desiree, whose mom was looking for her. She had a sweet smile with a small space between her two front teeth and soft dimples. On Christmas Eve, she was sold by her trafficker through Backpage and then found beaten and stabbed to death in a Chicago garage.[1]

ROUND 2

Our first court appearance was on January 8, 2017, in Department 8 in front of Judge Lawrence Brown, a seasoned and well-respected jurist with a prior career as a prosecutor. The defense was furious. They accused us of vindictive prosecution and abuse of process and all sorts of terrible violations I had never heard of before. They couldn't believe we had filed a new case in front of a new judge, instead of filing an appeal, and that the whole process was going to start over. They were especially offended that I'd filed the case two days before Christmas. Even the jolly Henzes were mad at us.

But I didn't even know what day it was, and I didn't care. My goal was to prosecute them as soon as I could. My complaint was ready on the twenty-third of December, so that's when I filed it. We didn't even arrest the defendants on the new charges, even though we could have. Instead we agreed to keep the bail conditions from the prior case in place and set a low-key arraignment date. I called the defense attorneys in advance to let them know about the filing and asked what day would be best for their schedules, something that we did not need to do. The only reason we had not charged money laundering before was because we didn't have the evidence and the analysis. Now, we were ready—or at least getting there.

Meanwhile, Attorney General Harris was sworn in as a US senator. During her first week on the job, she was sitting on the committee that was investigating Backpage—she'd be cross-examining Carl Ferrer before I got a chance to! Her prior chief deputy, now chief of staff to the senator, called me for tips. And one morning at 5:00 a.m. California time, Senator Harris called me as she was headed to the hearing and I was walking into my gym. As usual, she got me off guard, out of the office, somewhere with loud noise and bad phone reception. It was nice checking in with her, and I was glad she still cared about the case. I told her I'd hold down the fort at DOJ and wished her good luck in the Senate. In the end, in typical fashion, the Backpage executives refused to testify and appealed the Senate's subpoenas for their records all the way up to the US Supreme Court.

The day the executives were supposed to testify, Backpage shut down the escort section of the site voluntarily. They posted a message claiming government censorship with links to various claims about our case and the Senate investigation. I didn't really care. They were no longer selling teenagers, and that was a victory.

A few weeks later, the US Senate released a scathing report on the subcommittee's investigation.[2] The report referenced our case and discussed the details of how the website worked, the way Backpage moderated the sites and content, and even the conversations Backpage executives had with the National Center for Missing & Exploited Children. Yiota had testified at the Senate hearing about thousands and thousands of missing kids who were being commercially sexually exploited through Backpage.

The evidence for our criminal case was even stronger and had been obtained by search warrant, without the defendants knowing or having opportunities to refuse to provide documents. We would not be relying on the Senate's report, but we hoped it would help the world see what was really happening. Rather than the barrage of news stories about our frivolous attack on the First Amendment, maybe the media would start writing about the plight of the kids who were being trafficked. And if the CDA was truly preventing law enforcement from taking down the world's biggest sex trafficker, perhaps this Senate investigation would convince Congress that it was time to change that law.

Because Kamala Harris left for the Senate before finishing her term as attorney general, Governor Jerry Brown appointed a new attorney general, Xavier Becerra. Becerra had a long list of accomplishments from his twenty-plus years in Congress, but I Googled his name with "human trafficking" and came up empty. He otherwise had a solid reputation and seemed supportive of our office's work, but would he be in favor of continuing to pursue the case? Had we gone so far out on a limb that he would suddenly come in and cut us off? What if he was funded by Silicon Valley dot-com companies that would mischaracterize our case and convince him to shut it down before we had a chance to brief him? Powerful interests were already lining up, in anticipation of a CDA amendment based on the Senate's report. Or what if the defense attorneys were able to get to him through progressive political fund-raising circles? Becerra could also just simply decide he didn't want to allocate resources to this case when the Special Crimes Unit could be doing other cases that better fit his platform. He had many priorities. He was laser focused on fighting newly elected President Trump and the federal administration on everything—California had already been dubbed the "State of Resistance," and he was leading the fight.

Meanwhile, I was finally working well with the feds. Kevin Rapp, a charismatic assistant United States attorney out of Arizona, had taken the case. Kevin was smart, diligent, and truly passionate about taking on Backpage. The case seemed to have finally fallen on the right desk at the right federal office. The Senate referral had given Kevin new momentum and extensive resources to pursue Backpage throughout the country. He and I were in frequent contact and were becoming fast friends. Brian and I were sharing evidence with the FBI and IRS, and based on their questions and requests, it seemed their case was finally moving forward, although not quickly enough!

In my mind, the feds had a much easier case than we did from the get-go. First of all, they weren't limited to any particular jurisdiction—they could file the case wherever they wanted to. Second, they had dedicated resources to do financial analysis, tax analysis, and money-laundering analysis. If they were able to identify assets, even overseas, they would be able to seize them.

Most significantly, the feds didn't have to contend with the CDA. The CDA specifically exempted *federal criminal law* from immunity along with state law that was not inconsistent. I had argued, unsuccessfully, that our criminal case was perfectly consistent with federal law, that the California pimping and sex-trafficking provisions were similar to those in federal law and were merely an exercise of the state's police power. "Why aren't the feds prosecuting it, then?" is what I heard over and over again. That's a damn-good question. But now, with the Senate report, the growing public pressure, and Kevin at the helm of the investigation, the feds were poised to do just that. And they would not get bogged down arguing about the CDA immunity when charging violations of federal criminal law.

I sat down with the federal team multiple times. I really appreciated Kevin's insights and his dedication to the case. He was great to work with and cared about my case as much as his. After the case got dismissed, I was dreading telling him what happened because I was just so disappointed. I remember him sending me an email: "Maggy, I was so crestfallen for you reading the news about your case. You are a profile in courage." It was kind and thoughtful and a welcome departure from the "we told you so" vibe I got from others. As long as Backpage would be shut down, I didn't care who landed the final blow. I was happy to be able to share my work with both Kevin and Texas, hoping that my efforts would not be in vain. I felt strongly that we were all on the same team.

But I still wanted to move my case forward, not knowing if and when anyone else would file charges. Before I had a chance to brief Attorney General Becerra and his executive team about our anti-sex-trafficking work and the pending high-profile cases, a reporter asked Becerra if he was going to continue to pursue the Backpage case. I don't know if he even knew about it at the time, but his response was perfect: "We are going to descend on Backpage with every weapon in our arsenal."

I was delighted and relieved. I dreaded a conversation in which I refused to dismiss the case and instead turned in my badge. That never happened. And instead I got the chance to sit down with Attorney General Becerra and learn for myself how smart, personable, and dedicated he is. He was very interested in pursuing human-trafficking cases and wanted to dedicate even more resources to the fight. I also had the opportunity to discuss the challenges of the Backpage prosecution and the way Judge Bowman had interpreted the Communications Decency Act. I explained that although I believed our new filing was on solid legal ground, to be sure this court and courts across the country allow law enforcement to go after those who facilitate sex trafficking, we should clarify the law to contain a specific exemption for state criminal prosecutions like this one. Specifically, attorney generals across the country were being asked to publicly support a bill to amend the Communications Decency Act to create a specific exception to the immunity shield for sex-trafficking cases. This was particularly meaningful from California's vantage point, since we were the ones struggling to prosecute Backpage and also the home state of the biggest platform companies. Not only did Attorney General Becerra agree to lead the charge among state attorney generals (eventually, fifty state attorney generals joined onto a support letter), he agreed to testify in support of the bill back in his old stomping grounds in Congress. He was the real deal.

When I was helping Attorney General Becerra prepare to testify, a funny thing came up: "I was in Congress in 1996, and I remember passing this law!" he said. "Thanks," I muttered sarcastically, momentarily forgetting that I was speaking to the attorney general. But we both started laughing. He recognized that in 1996, it was beyond anyone's wildest imagination that this law would later act as a shield for sex traffickers. And this fact made Attorney General Becerra the perfect person to help fix this giant loophole and explain to his former colleagues in Congress why the CDA should not shield sex traffickers from criminal liability. Yiota was carefully tracking the bill and kept me informed as it made its way through the House and Senate, slowly garnering support and some very vocal opposition. It would be at least a year of amendments, committee hearings, and political sparring, but eventually there would be a final vote.

Meanwhile, we continued to litigate our money-laundering case in front of Judge Brown. Brian had been working on other cases for months now, assigned to a new unit focused on gambling enforcement, but he kept track of our progress. He compared us to gum on the bottom of a shoe—no matter how hard the Backpage attorneys tried, they couldn't get rid of the charges. "Still stuck to the bottom of the shoe," I'd text him after each court appearance, as the case survived through motion after motion, court hearings, arguments, supplemental briefs, all the way through the spring and into the summer.

In the first half of 2017, we were justifying the new filing and responding to defense motions about procedural malfeasance. Essentially, they argued that we could not refile the case and that it should be transferred to Judge Bowman to determine whether it cured the defects that caused the first dismissal. In their view, obviously it did not. I remember Jim Grant arguing during one court hearing, "This complaint is even worse, even more defective, your honor!" *How did I make it even more defective?* I wondered. "This is a new case, with new charges, based on new evidence, your honor." In addition to money laundering, we had added more victims and special allegations to explain why we were outside the CDA's immunity right on the face of the complaint. It didn't make sense to go to Judge Bowman because he handled the in-custody arraignment calendar, from a different courthouse attached to the jail. Because we did not rearrest the defendants, we were in the main courthouse on the out-of-custody calendar. This had been assigned by the clerk, and there was nothing I could do, even if I wanted to.

But I also would not oppose going back to Judge Bowman. The prosecutor does not get to pick the judge. There is a mechanism for filing a preemptory challenge on a judge you don't believe can be fair to you or your case, but the Attorney General's Office had a policy against exercising this legal right. Known as "Jerry's Rule," affectionately named after the chief of the Criminal Division at the time, the idea was that we show our strength and our faith in the judicial system by trying our case in whatever courtroom it lands. We don't pick and choose. We put on our evidence, argue our case, and let justice prevail. I was good with following the rule.

I didn't have any animosity toward Judge Bowman. He was patient and thoughtful and seemed genuinely troubled by what he perceived to be the state of the law. But I was frustrated that I wasn't able to convince him to let me present evidence that Backpage helped create the ads. He seemed deferential to the private defense lawyers, and I didn't know whether the money-laundering charges would help him see that the defendants should not be shielded from criminal liability or whether he would become impatient with our persistence in bringing out-of-town website owners to his over-burdened courtroom. Ultimately, I thought that if I gave him a better hook, we would prevail, and it was a risk I was willing to take.

But Judge Brown decided it would not be proper to send the case to Judge Bowman. He did take judicial notice of the record of the first case, including all of the filings and Judge Bowman's opinion. Based on Judge Brown's questions about the money-laundering charges, we amended the complaint. We wanted the charges to be as explicit as possible about the fact that we were not relying on any of their functions as a publisher. In addition to accusing the defendants of laundering pimping and commercial-sex proceeds, we accused them of laundering assets that were fraudulently obtained. The fraud was completely separate from the website operation and their claims about being publishers. This resulted in more motions about their due process rights and speedy-trial rights. I was also pushing for a speedy trial—there was nothing I wanted more than to get the case to a jury. But that obviously was not what they wanted. They wanted the charges dismissed. And they certainly didn't want the victims to have their day in court.

Even though the dismissal motions were up in the air, we were continuing to build and prepare our case. We were now subpoenaing additional bank records and attempting to fill in gaps with data obtained via search warrant from Amazon Web Services, where Backpage stored transaction data. We knew that Backpage itself also probably had the data we needed, but we hadn't been able to obtain it during our search-warrant execution in Texas.

Since we hadn't charged Backpage as a corporate entity in the case, one day in court Reye attempted to subpoena the data directly from the company. It was before court had started, and I was sitting at counsel table. Liz McDougall, Backpage's corporate lawyer, was sitting in the courtroom audience.

Reye went and sat behind her and tapped her on the shoulder. "Excuse me, ma'am, are you Liz McDougall?" Reye was wearing slacks and a shirt, and McDougall clearly had no idea who he was.

"Yes, I am," she said, seeming almost flattered that someone knew who she was.

Reye then handed her the subpoena.

Suddenly she frowned and started to quickly explain why she wasn't the appropriate person.

Reye handed her another piece of paper, a declaration she had submitted in a civil case stating under penalty of perjury that she was Backpage's legal representative. Reye asked— knowing the answer—"Are you saying you're not Backpage's legal representative?"

McDougall slumped into her chair, and Reye winked at me, just as Judge Brown took the bench. The defense team was now huddling around McDougall, as Judge Brown loudly called the case, adding, "Are we ready, counsel?" at the gaggle of defense lawyers. He ultimately did not address the subpoena during court that day, but he made clear that our investigation could continue and rejected the defense's claim that the prosecution should cease any investigative activity pending the outcome of the dismissal motions. They could not stop us from pursuing the case, at least not then.

After a few more rounds of briefing, contentious arguing, and more briefing, Judge Brown set a "final" hearing for July 14, 2017, on the defense dismissal and other motions.

I prepared meticulously. A brilliant appellate prosecutor named Steve Oetting out of our San Diego office had taken an interest in the case and offered to help us brief and argue some of the thorniest legal issues. I felt that having him come to court to argue certain aspects of our case would be impressive to Judge Brown, who seemed taken by Grant. Grant would talk nonstop for several minutes at a time, citing a bevy of cases and reading misleading snippets to make it sound like he easily won on all issues the court asked about.[3] If it was a football game, he would win the time-of-possession battle by a landslide, and he had already won in Judge Bowman's court.

I tried to be succinct and answer the court's questions directly. I never felt that shutting down each of his arguments and countering each of the cases or talking for the longest period of time was the best strategy or even an option for me. My focus was explaining the prosecution's charges and theory and refocusing the court on the fact that it was a dismissal motion and our actual case had yet to be heard. But sometimes I wasn't thorough enough and probably oversimplified the issues. I was concerned that Judge Brown would not have the patience for me to pick apart all of Grant's arguments or explain why each case was being relied on erroneously. I didn't want to provoke a "We get it, Ms. Krell. Time to move on."

Perhaps it was because Judge Brown was familiar with me or because I was the prosecutor and he had higher expectations. Or it could have been because I was continuing to defend the pimping charges that he had already rejected in his mind. I also had been putting off eye-doctor appointments for years, so I couldn't confirm whether his facial expressions were in fact scowls. But when Grant rambled and rambled, Judge Brown seemed to listen intently, unbothered by the time-suck or the inaccuracies in his argument. He almost seemed enamored of Grant, even when Grant was mis-citing cases and lobbing inflammatory accusations at the prosecution. Judge Brown and Grant would even sometimes quip little jokes back and forth.

I never wanted to admit the fact that older white men tend to listen to each other and give each other the benefit of the doubt, but of course it crossed my mind. Bowman, Brown, and Grant were similarly aged, well-educated white guys. I was the odd woman out.

I thought of the time that Dave Druliner and I were late to a pre-trial hearing in Susanville: he had danced his way through, charming the judge and somehow escaping his wrath. I would have been skewered. While I enjoyed watching Dave melt the judge, I knew I couldn't have gotten away with it. And I still couldn't. Steve Oetting from San Diego could be in that club, though. An older white guy with instant credibility—Judge Brown would automatically listen to Steve, and it would be a perfect change of pace.

Don't get me wrong, Steve was also a terrific lawyer and so generous with his time and wisdom—I was grateful for his help on the case. He and I would discuss the case intensely sometimes—he would push for brilliant arguments that he thought would be beneficial to make for an appeal but I didn't think would necessarily fly in Judge Brown's court. He would say that he was reverse engineering my case to make good case law down the road. "I just want to go to trial on these facts and shut these guys down," I would argue. I would tell him what happened in court, and he would get frustrated on my behalf, trying to coach me through the next round of briefing.

"Did you explain the concept of *scienter*?"

"What, you mean criminal intent?" I responded.

"Yes, but you should explain it as *scienter*."

"But no one uses that word, Steve. It will sound weird." To be honest, I didn't even know how to pronounce *scienter*, and it sounded funny when he said it.

The concept was crucial for our case, though—we needed to make sure the court understood that the crimes we alleged contained a criminal intent requirement. That criminal knowledge or intent is what separated our case from other First Amendment cases in which the publisher did not know what was being published or the bookstore owner did not know that one of his shelves contained one book with a pornographic image on one page. This was not a strict liability case. We hadn't charged the Backpage owners over a handful of images or something they had inadvertently published—we charged them because their entire site was *intentionally* dedicated to an illegal purpose. This point was crucial and hadn't been sinking in with either Judge Bowman or Judge Brown.

I discussed the conversation that Steve and I had with Randy to see if she knew the term *scienter* and whether she thought my using that word in court would help. But my attempting to say *scienter* in the same way Steve had said it sent us both into an uncontrollable fit of giggles. "I definitely don't think you should say that in court," she concluded.

On July 17, I did my usual precourt routine of listening to Eminem's "Lose Yourself" in my office before grabbing Randy to walk to court for our "final" hearing. This time, we also had Steve with us; he was talkative and excited to finally be in the courtroom in a case he had been backseat-driving on for months. We filed into the courtroom and up to our usual spot at counsel table, this time making room for our additional lawyer. I greeted the defense lawyers and started arranging my carefully constructed binders containing all of our briefings, cases, and notes.

When Judge Brown took the bench and called the case, I introduced Steve as Mr. Oetting to the court, explaining that he was an appellate expert from San Diego and had even represented the Attorney General's Office in some of the cases the parties had been discussing. Steve was firm and articulate, skillfully weaving through Grant's arguments and poking holes in every single one. Judge Brown did seem to take notice and show deference to Steve. Judge Brown would lob questions, and Steve would answer them, almost like a professor. Kind of in response to a question but also veering in his own direction a bit, Steve started explaining the concept of *scienter* to the court, repeating the word over and over again. All I knew is I could *not* look at Randy.

We tag-teamed more questions from the court. At one point in the hearing, Grant misstated several facts about how the business operated, giving me the opportunity to read from emails the defendants had sent to each other. I read an email in which Carl Ferrer told his executive team that they needed to change Backpage company names and billing descriptors in order to deceive the banks. By this time, all of the major banks and credit-card companies had refused to do business with Backpage because of its involvement in human trafficking. But Backpage created a web of other shell companies, corporate names, and websites, so that the banks would not realize they were doing business with Backpage and would continue to process its transactions.

> THE COURT: Can I ask you a question?
>
> MS. KRELL: Yes.
>
> THE COURT: Billing descriptors. Is that for the benefit, though, of the person whose credit card statement they get so it doesn't show something that might be embarrassing to a family member who might be opening up the mail, for example? Isn't that what a billing descriptor is? It's the thing that shows up on your statement?
>
> MS. KRELL: That is what counsel states in his argument, but his client Mr. Ferrer seems to think otherwise. In an e-mail dated September 12, 2013, the defendant says that, "Cardholder bank block based on billing descriptor, phone number, and corporation names. We need a different corporation name for both Arizona Bank and Trust and a different one for Esquire. It would give us the ability to route Chase and Bancorp transactions to them in the event that they catch on to the BIN and the routing numbers. AZ Bank and Trust and Esquire still won't work with our Chase or Bancorp transactions or any future bank like Chase trying to block us unless we use a different corporation."[4]

Grant then jumped from his table, flagging the fact that this wasn't an evidentiary hearing and objecting to my sharing evidence with the court. Grant also argued that all of the transactions we charged were processed successfully, and therefore the banks had obviously approved the transactions. I managed to get in one more damning email, in which, in response to a question about the banks, Ferrer wrote, "I doubt any of the banks know what we are doing."

MR. GRANT: I have the same objection, Your Honor.

THE COURT: Duly noted. Thank you.

MS. KRELL: The point being, Your Honor, the evidence will show that when the transactions were successful, it was because the defendants' fraud was successful. And when the banks knew, the defendants were blocked.

I then went on to discuss the pimping counts, giving it one more last shot. As I was arguing, the defense team was loudly whispering back and forth, and Grant seemed to be making inside jokes to Judge Brown. Judge Brown would interrupt me periodically to ask an obscure question, and then as I was answering it, Grant would interrupt with his own answer.

"The heart of the prosecution's case is the exploitation of these victims, charged in counts 28–40," I argued, and the defense's theory rests on the ads being protected because they are a legitimate exercise of speech. But nothing about Backpage was ever legitimate.

The Backpage website appeared to feature a variety of classified services, but its single purpose and overwhelming source of income was its adult section. Though titled "Escort," the advertisements therein were invariably for prostitution.

Nearly every ad featured virtually naked pictures, text describing sexual acts, and accompanying fees for sexual services. Sometimes this language was coded, sometimes it was blatant, but it universally connected traffickers, pimps, and prostitutes to purchasers of commercial sex. Defendants were well-aware of the site's illicit purpose, the extent of their illegal proceeds, and the fact that those being advertised were often sex trafficking victims, many of them children, including the children charged in our case. These aren't legal services . . . They cannot be protected by the CDA.[5]

I explained the problems with the First Amendment line of cases the defense was relying on. Unlike the cases on which they relied, this wasn't protected speech or political speech. They weren't Vietnam protestors or unwitting bookstore owners. They were owners of an online brothel that trafficked children. They were not being prosecuted for speech at all—it was their *conduct*—receiving money from commercial sex—that caused the felony charges.

Our other strategy was to focus on money laundering and take the ads and the pimping entirely out of the equation. This was a fraud case in which the defendants had lied in order to obtain financial services—no ads, no third-party website postings, just a corrupt fraud scheme in which defendants deceived their business partners. When charging money laundering, you must also identify an underlying offense that the defendants laundered proceeds from or laundered proceeds to propel. Pimping and commercial sex were the obvious crimes, but instead we used bank fraud on several of the counts in order to completely disassociate from any website activity. Bank fraud is a federal offense, and we were in state court; but the California money-laundering statute allows you to rely on any felony, in any jurisdiction. This of course was also a new theory that caused many more questions, argument about preemption, and assertions by Grant and the team that the prosecution was trying to skirt the CDA. We answered the questions and explained our case as well as we could. We were trying to prove that the defendants' criminal operation was entirely outside the bounds of CDA protection.

The oral arguments lasted hours. Finally, a wearied Judge Brown had heard enough and said he would take the matter under submission and issue a written ruling. *Uh-oh*, I thought, *another written ruling*. But he also set a court date for August 23, 2017. The defense attorneys asked whether their clients had to be there and made a big deal about their busy travel schedules. "Perhaps if the case is being dismissed, there's no reason these gentlemen need to come all the way to Sacramento again," Grant suggested. But Judge Brown, without hinting in either direction, said that the parties should plan on being in court and that he'd be issuing a written ruling in advance.

After the hearing, I planned to meet with some of the victim advocates who had attended court. My dear friend Ashlie Bryant, whom I had been working with on a human-trafficking prevention curriculum, attended the hearing. Before joining her at a nearby restaurant, I needed to run back to my office to drop off my mass of binders and quickly shoot out an email outlining what happened in court for our bosses and the many people interested in the case. I somehow lost Randy in the shuffle of people getting out of court. She was probably scrambling to get to day care on time and our ringer from San Diego had a flight to catch. So, I could not immediately lament to the team about all the things I should have said in court.

Meeting up with Ashlie was always a treat. She understood the big picture and was relentlessly optimistic and had a contagious positive energy. She had gone from volunteering in one high school in her neighborhood to talk to students about sex trafficking to building a hugely successful national nonprofit called 3Strands Global Foundation to train students in all schools about human trafficking.[6] Together we were working with other stakeholders to develop a model curriculum that could be adopted, and adapted as needed, by teachers across the country. The goal was to empower kids to protect themselves and each other from the danger of human trafficking. We saw far too many cases in which a vulnerable middle-school girl would go on a date, get taken out to eat, be showered with gifts and attention, and then be either suddenly forced into the commercial sex trade or manipulatively coaxed into "making some money" for someone. There were warning signs all along the way, and we believed that if kids were better educated, we could prevent many of the cases from happening.

Back at work, I continued to collect evidence against the Backpage defendants, comb through documents, and ready our case for trial (which, in my fantasy world, was imminent). Darrell Early, our team's forensic auditor, was now working with Bassem to streamline our money-laundering evidence. He was a super-smart former IRS auditor and a welcome addition to the team. After everything we had been through, I insisted in ensuring that we were actually well prepared to go forward, just in case the defense opted to move quickly.

Literally every day in August, I received at least one call or text from someone asking whether we received a ruling. Bassem would call to tell me that he noticed we were twenty-seven cents off in count 18 or to tell me he noticed something else suspicious in Backpage's transactions with a particular bank during a particular week. He might have been just trying to calm his own nerves or test my commitment and confidence in our ability to move the case forward. I went back and forth between texting Yiota and texting Brian. It felt like waiting for Flight 21 all over again, but this time I didn't know whether Carl Ferrer would be on it. The press office would call to make sure I hadn't heard anything, as reporters were constantly calling them to check in. Police officers from other jurisdictions, prosecutors from various offices throughout the country, victim advocates, and lawyers for victims were closely following the case and calling me to make sure they had not missed it. At this point, even my supportive parents and in-laws were curious and would ask, "How's that one case going? Are you still waiting on the judge?" The whole nation seemed to be watching.

Kevin Rapp called to check in. "What do you think is taking so long?" he asked after I expressed frustration about still not having a ruling just a couple of days before the August 23 court date. "Yeah, Kevin, what is taking so long?" I chided back, making a not so subtle jab at the feds for not having filed their case yet. "This would be the perfect week to do it," I continued. "I can even tell you where they are all going to be on August 23, so you won't have to spend weeks doing surveillance and chasing them down all over the world like I did!" Kevin laughed. "I wish . . . ," he said.

I tried to stay busy—it's not like I didn't have dozens of other cases to prosecute, warrants to review, investigations to assign out. And my kids were out of school for summer, so I was coordinating carpools from half-day camps and constantly fielding calls from them about how their lunches were too small and they were *starving* and bored at home. But the days ticked by, and still nothing from Judge Brown and his clerk. I reread the transcript from the July hearing a dozen times—he definitely said he was issuing a written ruling in advance of the August court date! But when?

JUDGMENT DAY

August 23 arrived, and still no ruling had been issued. There was no more "before." We would find out whether we could prosecute the owners of Backpage with the rest of the world in a packed courtroom at 1:30 p.m. on August 23, 2017. Randy and I walked to the courthouse together. As usual, Randy didn't seem stressed at all. She was perfectly dressed and chipper. She chattered about her kids and the various colds and ear infections they'd picked up at day care despite it being summer. "Eli always seems to have an ear infection, and what's with these summer colds?" I wasn't really listening. I was both extremely stressed out and emotionally numb at the same time. I could feel my entire purse vibrating from a bevy of phone calls. I knew it was people wanting to know about Backpage, and it didn't calm my nerves.

Just as we walked down the hallway to Department 8, the bailiff unlocked the courtroom door. Randy and I cruised past a crowd of people and up to counsel table. I managed to make small talk with a deputy district attorney who was already in the courtroom. I caught Reye's eye in the back of the room, and he gave me a little smile, like he already knew something. He was sitting with Jackie Salvi, our team's trusted paralegal and my emotional rock throughout the case. Then I noticed that the clerk had an enormous stack of papers on her desk. Before Judge Brown came out of chambers to take the bench, the clerk said in a shrill but loud voice to a packed courtroom, "I'm going to hand out this ruling in an orderly manner. When I call your name, please come get your copy." She then started reading the names of all the defense attorneys. There were still lots of them. Each suited lawyer walked to the clerk and got his or her copy. The defendants each got their own. Lacey, Larkin, and Ferrer sat silently reading, guarded by their cluster of lawyers. Randy might have still been talking about whether her toddler Eli needed ear tubes, but I was staring at the defendants. And from their sour faces, I knew what the ruling was long before "Maggy Krell" got called.

When Randy and I finally got our copies, we were elated. She started at the beginning, but I flipped to the last page of the ruling. The pimping charges had been dismissed, but all the money-laundering and conspiracy charges held up. It was enough to put each defendant behind bars for more than twenty years, and it would shut down the entire business. No more Backpage!

I texted Yiota from counsel table, "We're still in! On money laundering and conspiracy!" She was happy and not concerned about the pimping charges getting tossed again—if anything, the ruling helped our attempt to change the CDA while still allowing us to move forward with serious felony charges that would shut down Backpage forever. She never said this directly, but she had been working so hard behind the scenes to change the law on the premise that it prevented law enforcement from going after the worst offenders in the industry, like Backpage. Our pimping charges being dismissed actually supported what the antitrafficking advocates wanted to do legislatively—a fix that would echo beyond just one judge in one courtroom or one website. Meanwhile, I just wanted to be able to move the case forward

and shut down Backpage once and for all. If we had to prove financial fraud and money laundering to close their criminal enterprise,
stop them from selling sex acts with teenagers, and finally hold
them accountable, so be it.

Judge Brown eventually made it to the bench. He called the chaotic courtroom to order and started reading sections of his ruling
out loud for the cameras:

> As amply briefed by the parties, federal law provides broad im-
> munity for internet service providers from both federal and state
> prosecutions. Indeed, the 9th Circuit federal appellate court has
> instructed such immunity be applied liberally. The underlying
> public policy is to permit, and promote, the robust growth of
> the internet by shielding internet providers from facing suit over
> the content created by those posting on their sites. If and until
> Congress sees fit to amend the immunity law, the broad reach of
> section 230 of the Communications Decency Act even applies
> to those alleged to support the exploitation of others by human
> trafficking.
>
> However, immunity afforded to internet service providers is
> not without limit. Even the most ardent defenders of a vigorous
> world wide web would have to concede that if a provider engaged
> in their own criminal acts, versus those of their customers,
> immunity must fail. And so it is in this case. While the charges
> relating to pimping will not be allowed to proceed, the offenses
> pertaining to allegations that the Defendants themselves
> engaged in financial crimes, to include bank fraud and money
> laundering to disguise their business dealings, will survive the
> demurrer stage.[7]

I sat quietly, showing no emotion while secretly doing backflips
inside.

After Judge Brown finished reading his ruling, he asked the
defense when they could come back to court for the preliminary

hearing date. They were frozen, not even reaching for their calendars. Usually it was a big ordeal: They would mutter about the travel and how busy they were, keynoting at a conference here and taking a case to the Supreme Court there. They would huddle together, hem and haw, argue among themselves about who had the busiest, most important schedule, consult with the clerk, and then finally emerge with a date. Randy and I would automatically agree, no matter what our calendars actually said we were supposed to be doing. Then we would argue back at the office about who would rearrange everything and how.

Jim Grant, with the wind still knocked out of him, stumbled toward the podium adjacent to counsel table. "How about the fifteenth," he stammered.

"That's actually a Saturday," I pointed out.

I offered the court a new date and suggested that I could coordinate with the defense team to ensure that it worked for everyone's schedule. If we found that it didn't, the parties would recalendar through the clerk's office. Judge Brown agreed and set the hearing, eager to have all the media, lawyers, and spectators out of his courtroom so that he could go back to his regular calendar of low-profile felony drug offenders.

Randy and I sat at the table, packing our notes and chatting with the deputy public defender as we watched a defeated Ferrer, Larkin, and Lacey slump out of the courtroom with their deflated lawyers. Once they were gone, we headed for the door, but there they were just outside the courtroom.

The defense team was talking to the press, of course: "All substantive charges against our clients have been dismissed. These are just financial, technical charges," they bluffed. But we knew the truth. The truth was that their legal strategy had just hit a brick wall and their clients were headed for prison.

Randy and I were headed for pizza and beer. I hadn't had lunch, and I still wanted to read the ruling. The press office and our bosses were calling, but the good news was already out. As we were walk-

Defendants and lawyers listening to Judge Brown's ruling (Courtesy of the *Sacramento Bee*)

ing down to K Street, I sent out a flurry of text messages to Carissa Phelps, Ashlie Bryant, Bassem Banafa, Jessica Owen, Steve Oetting, and the many other people invested in the case. "How the hell did we do this, Maggy?" said Randy when we sat down at Pizza Rock. "I think you should get Eli the ear tubes—he won't have an ear infection all the time and will be able to pronounce tricky words like *scienter* when he grows up." We both started laughing. Within minutes, Brian, Reye, Jackie, Darrell, and the rest of the squad showed up. It was a great moment to celebrate, even though we still had a ways to go.

10

THE BREAKDOWN

SOME of the people in my department wanted us to appeal the dismissal of the pimping charges. Steve Oetting felt there were cognizable arguments about the extent of CDA's protection from the enforcement of criminal laws. With his help, we had laid a strong record and had made unaddressed arguments about state police powers to enforce laws that were consistent with federal criminal law. There wasn't case law directly governing this situation, and we had developed the right set of facts to inch an appellate court toward a favorable opinion, which could positively impact other prosecutions down the road.

Our office had successfully prosecuted a different internet service provider for extortion. The defendant, Kevin Bollaert, had allowed users to post intimate photos of their exes without consent and then charged money to the exes, through a different website, to take the intimate photos down. This was a trending new form of sexual harassment, labeled "revenge porn" but more accurately described as cyber exploitation, since it involved the nonconsensual sharing of private photographs to shame the victim and potentially enrich defendants like Bollaert. In that case, the appellate court agreed with our prosecution theory that Bollaert was being prosecuted for the *act* of committing extortion, not just third-party expression on a website platform.[1] Prosecuting Backpage on a content-creation theory was the next logical step, and the appellate attorneys wanted to take it up. There was also still the lingering argument that the defendants were not protected publishers since they had exploited the images and used them on other sites for their own financial gain, without the victims' permission.

But appealing the dismissal of the pimping charges would probably put the rest of the case on hold. And there was also the risk that an appellate court, even more removed from the realities of sex trafficking than the trial court, would side with the defense wholeheartedly and even dismiss the money-laundering charges. But my biggest objection to appealing Judge Brown's ruling was that I didn't want to slow down the case. Sex trafficking had now migrated from the shuttered escort section to other portions of Backpage. Children were still being sold, and that needed to stop. The only way to shut it down completely was to obtain a felony conviction or obtain a warrant to virtually seize the site. We gained momentum with our ruling, and I wanted to push the gas, move the case forward, get a conviction, and shut down this despicable operation once and for all. My colleagues understood where I was coming from and agreed that we should keep moving forward, taking the quickest path toward shutting down the site. We did not file an appeal.

After our judgment, court in Department 8 felt different. Jim Grant and Judge Brown seemed to be less chummy, and the court's patience in general seemed to be dwindling. The tables had turned. The defense team also seemed to be divided. The lawyers were not all sitting together, and Grant was no longer the spokesperson for all three defendants. The defense team was still inundating us with motions to quash subpoenas, discovery demands, and other litigious requests. They certainly were not rolling over; but they lacked a cohesive defense strategy, and there seemed to be tension among them about how to proceed.

Then the Bay Area criminal defense attorneys asked us for a meeting. They wanted to better understand our case and the evidence against their clients. Randy hesitated. "This is a ploy. Whatever we tell them, they will use against us. We don't have time for their mind games. We need to finish producing the discovery and respond to their other motions." I had done meetings like this in big cases before. Sometimes if you show the defense attorneys the most damning pieces of evidence, it allows them to go back to their clients, set expectations, and propose resolving the case. But in this case, the defendants were "true believers." They would never see what they were doing as a crime. And there was no way in the world they would agree to go to prison for it. Lacey had the "HOLD FAST" tattoo on his knuckles still. Larkin and Lacey had been in it from the beginning and would fight through the end—they left the news empire they'd created to focus solely on developing and fighting for Backpage. In their demented world, they were fighting for free speech against government intrusion.

But what about Ferrer? I wondered. He made less money and had more criminal exposure. Most of the emails were from him. He did all the work. He was younger than Larkin and Lacey and hadn't been with them from the beginning. He was just a tech guy, doing all the grunt work, who worked his way up, all the way to the top of a criminal enterprise.

As a professional courtesy, I invited the defense team to meet with us. Grant couldn't make it. I was actually nervous about the meeting that Randy didn't want to have. I went from saying it would be no big deal to spending an inordinate amount of time creating a PowerPoint, which meant bothering Jackie to rent a projector and other equipment from the litigation support unit. And it wasn't just a PowerPoint using words. I wanted to impose images of emails from our database to walk the defense through the evidence. I then decided I needed more help from Bassem and Darrell to make sure I could crisply explain all of the complicated financial computations that went into the money-laundering transaction amounts. The worst thing would be for them to ask a question that I couldn't answer or be able to call BS on some aspect of our case. We had to assume they knew what we had, since it was mostly from their clients. Their clients probably explained to them what we would never be able to prove and probably gave them ideas for ways to expertly quiz us to determine what we had on them and what our weaknesses were. Randy's idea of not doing the meeting was gaining fast appeal, but I couldn't cancel last minute—that would be even worse.

So the attorneys came to our office as scheduled. We walked through our money-laundering charges during the meeting. Using the PowerPoint, we discussed the charges in detail and previewed some of our strongest pieces of evidence: emails from Ferrer to Larkin explaining how he created shell companies to thwart the major banks; emails from Larkin mocking efforts to combat sex trafficking; screenshots of Backpage manipulating financial transactions; notes from what Lacey said to the CEO of the National Center for Missing & Exploited Children. Randy chimed in, giving additional details and driving home our points. Her delivery was confident. She articulately explained why some of the defense claims would not be viable and simplified complex piles of emails. It was the kind of presentation that would show the lawyers that if they went to trial, their clients would be convicted.

I could tell we had made an impact on them, especially Carl Ferrer's attorney, who was audibly groaning as I read her client's emails out loud. In addition to being represented by Grant, each defendant had his own attorney. Normally when there are codefendants, each has his or her own lawyer. It was unusual for Grant to represent all three defendants, in addition to the corporation, since there could have easily been a conflict of interest between the defendants. The defendants may have waived the conflict or felt that since they each had his own representation in addition to Grant, there was not an issue.

In any event, without Grant in the room, Ferrer's attorney, whose sole job was to look out for the interests of Ferrer (not the other defendants or the corporation), saw the mountain of incriminating emails with Ferrer's name on them and was quickly realizing that Ferrer would be the fall guy. The air was thick with discomfort as we methodically laid bare his guilt, charge by charge, count by count. There was another sigh from Ferrer's lawyer as I flipped to one particularly troubling email in which Ferrer bragged about being able to deceive Chase by obtaining new bank identification numbers.

The charges against Ferrer were easiest to prove. Larkin and Lacey were less active on email, less involved in day-to-day operations, and seemingly more evasive. They even scraped their name off Backpage by "selling" the company to Ferrer, but kept such a lopsided loan that they continued to receive all of the profits without technically owning the company.

Ferrer, on the other hand, did the work. His fingerprints were all over every aspect of the business, even though it was Larkin and Lacey's idea. And Ferrer and his attorney realizing this may have gotten their wheels turning.

At the very next court appearance, Ferrer fired Grant. Grant's law firm had been with Backpage since the beginning. Grant and his team had successfully defended Backpage against civil suits and even had a hand in suing the Cook County sheriff to shut down an investigation. For the first time now, Ferrer was being represented by only one law firm, with the single interest in representing him. Grant would remain on the case but only on behalf of the other defendants. Ferrer was on his own.

Ferrer's lead lawyer isolated me in the hallway after court and said we should talk one-on-one. This usually only means one thing: plea deal. But there were still many, many challenges to overcome. Kevin and the feds were still working on a case, and even though I had not heard from Kirsta in a bit, I was sure Texas was not far behind either. My twenty-seven felonies in California might have been the least of Ferrer's problems.

Meanwhile, the bill titled SESTA (Stop Enabling Sex Trafficking Act) to amend the Communication's Decency Act was gaining steam in Congress. It was eventually cosponsored by a bipartisan coalition of twenty-seven senators. The bill was complicated. Initially, what I had pitched was just a simple fix that would clarify what I already argued to be the case: the CDA cannot be used as a shield from criminal enforcement. In other words, someone who commits a crime and harbors criminal intent can be prosecuted, even if the means of committing that crime was a website. The bill was more limited, in that it did not extend to all crimes, just human trafficking. But the change was also broader in that it applied to civil as well as criminal complaints. This would allow victims to privately sue an internet service provider that aided in their victimization.

Regardless, the bill clearly created an exception to CDA immunity for websites that engaged in sex trafficking—websites like Backpage. We would avoid using it retroactively as that would provoke other constitutional challenges, but it would be a game changer moving forward. If it actually passed and was signed, that would be a miracle. Powerful tech giants were stacking up against it and lobbying hard. If I got a felony conviction, that would be another miracle. And if the site was permanently shut down, that would be a third miracle. My sticky note from all those years ago would have done its job.

While all this was going on, and Backpage's fate still up in the air, the CEO of Planned Parenthood reached out to ask if I had any ideas about whom she could hire as chief counsel in California. Apparently, she wanted to hire me. I hadn't thought about leaving the DOJ and certainly wouldn't do so with Backpage pending. We were still in the early throes of litigation; we didn't even have a trial set, let alone a conviction. It was an intriguing opportunity and a mission I respected greatly, but I still felt as though I had unfinished business at DOJ.

And I loved being a prosecutor. I was shifting in my career from being a scrappy, in-the-trenches lawyer to being a supervisor and a mentor, dedicating more time to helping others develop than to my own cases. I thought often of my late mentor, Dave Druliner, and his last request to me: to spread what I had learned. I was honored to be training up the next generation of prosecutors to be better than I ever was. It was a tremendous privilege to be able to have such a role in another's life and to be working within a supportive department doing impactful work.

Looking back fifteen years, it was amazing how far the antitrafficking movement had come. When I started my career as a prosecutor in 2003, sex trafficking wasn't even defined in the Penal

Code, and vulnerable teenagers were going to jail for prostitution. While there was still work to be done, officers were trained on recognizing human trafficking; it became illegal, at least in California, to arrest minors for prostitution; and law enforcement was working with victim advocates to take a trauma-informed approach to investigations. Significant changes were finally coming to fruition to create a more just world for survivors.

The curriculum I had worked on with Ashlie Bryant and the other nonprofits was being rolled out in school districts throughout the state. Ashlie had secured grant funding and was rapidly expanding the program's reach. Meanwhile, she and I pushed together to pass a first-of-its-kind law in California—one that requires public school students to receive prevention education so that students will be empowered to protect themselves and each other from human traffickers.

Tasha, one of the victims from the Jordan case, called out of the blue one day. She wanted me to know that she was doing better. She had reenrolled in school, gotten a job at Home Depot, and wanted help getting her tattoos removed, the ones on her wrist and neck that said "Andrew" and "Jordan," respectively. We talked about this during a meeting before the trial—it was a vestige of her enslavement that was still holding her back. Every time she looked at her own arm, she was reminded of her trauma. Every time someone asked her about her tattoos, she had to answer in some way that never felt good. And it probably prevented her from getting other jobs. During a pretrial meeting, I'd mentioned to her that I knew of a place that would remove those tattoos for her, and she wouldn't have to pay anything. We had pictures of the tattoos—it's not like we needed them for trial. But she wasn't ready. We booked an appointment, and she didn't show up. She also was scared it would hurt like hell—and I couldn't argue with her on that.

But this time when she called, nearly two years after that initial meeting we had, she sounded confident and ready. She was the brave survivor who had stood up to her abuser in court. Her abuser was in prison, and she was pursuing her own goals. And now, in a courageous effort to truly leave him behind, she was ready to get rid of the tattoos that had branded her. I connected Tasha to a victim advocate in LA who would be taking her to a special dermatologist to either cover or remove the tattoos, free of charge. There would never be a moment when Tasha or any of the other trafficking survivors would be "all better." The suffering inflicted by human traffickers doesn't go away. The trauma lasts a lifetime, and healing is a journey. But Tasha was well on her way.

Toward the end of 2017, over a year after we had first filed the Backpage case and orchestrated Ferrer's arrest in Houston, his attorney called me. She wanted another meeting, but this time, she was asking me if I could pull together the feds and Texas. She wanted to explore a global resolution. No attorney in their right mind would advise their client to take a plea that would resolve charges in one jurisdiction without knowing what criminal liability awaited in another. I knew that Kevin and Kirsta were both working feverishly on their respective cases. I didn't know whether they would be amenable to having a conversation about this before they had even filed criminal charges. But what was particularly enticing to me was the fact that Ferrer owned Backpage. Because Larkin and Lacey had transferred the company over to him in the sham sale that made him owner on paper but gave them the majority of the profit via the loan terms, Ferrer now had control over the corporation. He could consent to searches, turn over documents, provide information about offshore bank accounts, and admit liability on behalf of the company. His cooperation could be extremely valuable. I was able to wrangle everyone together for a meeting. I did not know what the outcome would be. Each prosecutor had their own interest in the case, their own bosses to appease, and their own estimation of how strong their case could be without any cooperation.

But in the meantime, I was getting interested in working for Planned Parenthood. I felt confident that Backpage was crumbling—that the last precarious Jenga block precluding its tower from tumbling down was about to get pulled by the feds. Larkin, Lacey, and Ferrer were barely defending themselves from my case, and the federal case that Kevin had been steadily building would be an unbearable blow. And I thought about the way Dave had trusted me with my first murder case a decade earlier. Stepping aside would leave room for Randy and others on my team to grow and lead. I knew that the case was in good hands with Randy. She was unflappable and would never cave. She would always be well prepared, and she was fit to tangle with Jim Grant and his arsenal of lawyers. Good thing we kept her name on the complaint!

With Backpage still in the air and not much I could share outside of DOJ, I decided to call Carissa. I had promised her I would stay with the case and do my best on the three goals—the complete shutdown of Backpage, the felony conviction, and the CDA law change. I knew we were close, but I still hadn't accomplished those goals. Meanwhile, Carissa had moved out of state and taken a sabbatical to focus on her own health and goals, but she stayed up-to-date on our progress and was always just a phone call away. I told her that I was thinking of leaving DOJ but that I didn't want to break the promise of following through on Backpage. "You definitely followed through," she said. "You took this case farther than anyone ever could, and you've made a powerful statement in doing so." Even though I felt unfinished, in her mind, the promise had already been fulfilled and the goal exceeded.

We discussed the human-trafficking movement more broadly and how far we had come over the past several years. She congratulated me on landing a new job, thanked me for all I had done, and blessed my decision to move on. We made a pact to keep working together. Carissa wanted to do more to address the legal rights of victims outside the criminal justice system, and I was determined to ensure that health care providers were well trained in identifying and providing support for trafficking victims.

It was still a hard decision. There was always one more case. Bassem and others were pushing me to investigate RubMaps, another site that had become the go-to for finding massage-parlor brothels. I was close to filing a first-of-its-kind labor-trafficking case against a swath of in-home care employers who had been victimizing immigrant workers. Plus, the success of our movement had finally translated into more resources for human-trafficking cases. How could I leave DOJ when the task force I had been begging for since 2012 was finally close to getting funded?

But I also really felt a calling toward Planned Parenthood. I read a study showing that 80 percent of trafficking victims seek medical care at some point while they are being trafficked—and not just through the emergency room: 70 percent visit a community clinic, a clinic like Planned Parenthood.[2] And I knew from experience with survivors how vital Planned Parenthood was to their daily lives. Traffickers often withheld condoms and birth-control pills to control and manipulate their victims. Planned Parenthood was a safe space where women could confidentially access reproductive health care, as well as emotional support. Trafficking victims trusted Planned Parenthood. It was a refuge of sorts. And yet, under President Trump, Planned Parenthood and its patients were under attack. I was interested in fighting for survivors in a new arena and addressing the public-health aspects of the human-trafficking epidemic. I was becoming acutely aware that all problems couldn't be adequately addressed by the criminal justice system and of the value of a public-health perspective in addressing crime. I was ready to tackle these issues from another corner of the ring and take on new challenges.

In April 2018, I texted Yiota that it felt like October 6, 2016, that crazy, glorious, three-day day when we arrested the defendants and stormed the Backpage headquarters. This time, though,

I wasn't in Texas. I was in Portland, Oregon, on a quick getaway weekend with my husband, Cary. We were touring around downtown in the rain, sampling beer and food, and had tickets to see *Hamilton* that night. But my phone didn't stop ringing, and my mind was still on Backpage. I texted Senator Harris, who was still following the case. "Bravo," she replied. I joked with Brian that if he needed to sell a couch, Backpage wouldn't be available. I found myself messaging Yiota again, saying to watch the news. And she knew exactly what I meant.

That day, President Trump signed the law creating an exception to the CDA for sex trafficking. No other website would be able to knowingly facilitate sex trafficking and claim immunity because of the CDA. A few days later, the feds announced the arrests of Lacey, Larkin, and other coconspirators who helped run Backpage.[3] In a joint operation, California, Texas, and the FBI seized the Backpage website completely. The website directed users to a screen indicating the site had been shut down by law enforcement. It was finally over. No more teenagers would ever be sold on that contemptible site.

By this time, I had been at my new job at Planned Parenthood about a month. I took a day off from work and, on Randy's request, went to Department 8 of the Sacramento Superior Court, Judge Brown's courtroom. In order to ensure the success of a complex and precarious operation involving multiple agencies, Randy had managed to keep the court hearing completely off the public radar. The other defendants were being held in federal custody in Arizona. But Carl Ferrer sat slumped in the mostly empty courtroom, next to his lawyer.

Judge Brown took the bench. He greeted me warmly and congratulated me on the new job. Then he called the case. I was sitting a couple of rows behind Randy as she forcefully read the felony charges that she would be proceeding on. It was surreal. The room was silent. A wilted, shamed, aged Ferrer stood up, ambled to the podium with his lawyers, and admitted to multiple counts of money laundering and conspiracy. "To the charge of money laundering as alleged in court 4, Mr. Ferrer, how do you plead?" "Guilty, sir." And so on. Ferrer had agreed to fully cooperate against the other defendants and forfeit the company's assets in exchange for a five-year prison sentence. He had already secretly pled guilty to federal charges the day before and given a full proffer, outlining every detail of Backpage's criminal operation. And his next stop would be Texas, where he would be pleading guilty to charges on Kirsta's case and cooperating on Texas's investigation. Randy had perfectly orchestrated the operation.

And, just like that, all three of my sticky-note goals were met. The law had been changed. The site was gone. Ferrer was a convicted felon, and the others were well on their way. Randy and I headed to our traditional post-court stop for pizza and beer. Brian and the rest of the team joined us. My former colleagues were asking all about my new job, but I was basking in the old one. It was an incredible accomplishment, years in the making, that many of us had worked so hard on. It was not only a victory for Randy, Brian, and me but a victory for all the brave survivors who had come forward over the years. Their stories mattered. They were victims. And their courage and persistence are what enabled us to take down Backpage. It was worth the fight.

Larkin and Lacey would continue to slog it out in court and fight against the asset seizures and state and federal charges. Their former CEO would continue to cooperate as a key government witness against them and their criminal enterprise. The case would continue to wind its way through state and federal court, spurring a vigorous debate about the protections that should be afforded to websites and occupying an army of zealous defense lawyers. When it was all tallied, the feds managed to seize about $200 million in assets from Backpage, money that will eventually be given to the victims through a restitution fund when the case is over.

And Backpage remained shut down.

Screenshot of the Backpage website after the shutdown

AFTERWORD

HUMAN TRAFFICKING IN THE POST-BACKPAGE ERA

ANDREA G. told me that when the website went down, she was out on the "track," the term frequently used to describe a neighborhood where people go to meet up for commercial sex "dates." All the "working girls," as they call themselves, were freaking out trying to figure out what had happened to Backpage and why. They couldn't believe Backpage was gone and didn't know how the world would function without it. Andrea told me she took it as a sign from God. She sobered up, ran away from her trafficker, found a safe living place, and got a job. We still keep in touch, and she insists that the demise of Backpage helped her and so many others realize that it had been an abusive trap that propelled and normalized their victimization.

A national research study showed that following the shutdown of Backpage, sex trafficking declined by more than 25 percent. The study found, based on analytical data, that demand had also been reduced. "Backpage's closure dealt a huge blow to the illicit world of online prostitution. Demand for prostitutes dropped 67 percent and search volume plunged 90 percent immediately after the site went offline, the report showed."[1]

Fewer victims were being trafficked. Fewer predators were on the prowl. The industry was less lucrative. But still, an epidemic has persisted. There is no shortage of street traffickers, vulnerable teenagers, and places for them to be exploited, whether in massage parlors, on new websites, or on street corners. This is not a problem we can arrest and prosecute ourselves out of. Don't get me wrong: we can and should hold sex traffickers accountable, and that's where law enforcement should focus its limited resources, as opposed to street-level prostitution busts. The way that law enforcement engages in these cases is critical. Officers must be well trained; investigations should be trauma-informed and culturally competent, and include mental health professionals and survivor support at every step. Officers should work closely with victim-service providers throughout the investigative process.

But aside from the criminal justice response, we need to address root issues on all sides of the equation: too often, victims experiencing pervasive poverty and homelessness are coerced into sex trafficking, which morphs into survival sex because they feel it is the only way they can survive. We need to invest in the creation of educational and job opportunities for those who are most at risk and have been historically disadvantaged. The disproportionate number of Black girls and women in the sex trade must be counteracted by investment in underserved neighborhoods and schools. There need to be fewer on-ramps and more off-ramps when it comes to the commercial sex trade. Survivors face particular challenges when seeking gainful employment because they have missed high school while being trafficked; they suffer from substance abuse, which was a key coping mechanism in surviving their exploitation; they are branded with tattoos, which disqualify them from some customer-service positions; they suffer medical conditions as a result of being trafficked; they suffer long-lasting mental health effects such as PTSD, depression, and anxiety, which can make it difficult to interact in workplace environments, respond to conflict, or perform under pressure; they have a criminal record; or they do not have a stable living environment. And these are just a few of the issues that need to be addressed to help a victim survive and permanently get out of the cycle of commercial sex.

Child victims present other unique challenges. Sex-trafficking victims are often targeted for recruitment because they are sexually or physically abused at home. They run from an abusive and violent home life, desperate for help, and become easy targets on the street.[2] They are particularly vulnerable because they are searching for emotional nourishment, affection, and attention, in addition to basic needs like food, clothing, and a place to stay. Predators have ways of finding them and fulfilling these needs while manipulating them into a life of coerced commercial sex. Sometimes traffickers will identify victims through social media, looking for clues such as risk-taking behavior, lack of parental presence and involvement, and an implied willingness on the part of the teenager to party, fit in, run away from home, or just meet new people. Vulnerability factors are further enhanced by failures in the child-welfare system. Juvenile hall and group homes that should be protected spaces for vulnerable children often serve as grounds for sex-trafficking recruitment, where victims are lured into commercial sex instead of protected from further abuse.

The prognosis for victims can be devastating. Many wind up in the criminal justice system on cases of their own. There is a well-documented pipeline from sexual abuse to prison, especially for young women.[3] Sex-trafficking victims often face lengthy prison sentences, while the trauma that they suffered as victims goes unaddressed. This has been disproportionately true for Black girls and women whose oppression in the sex trade dates back to slavery. Current data reflect that Black girls are far more likely to be arrested for prostitution and are disproportionately represented in the juvenile justice population.[4] Take the case of Cyntoia Brown Long, for example, a sex trafficking survivor who bravely went public with her story. Celebrity interest from Kim Kardashian and others catapulted her experiences into national news—at age sixteen, she received a life sentence for killing a predator. Following public pressure, the Tennessee governor commuted her sentence to fifteen years.[5] But the publicity her story received and the ensuing sentencing commutation were possibly the most exceptional aspects of her case. There are numerous women in prison throughout the country whose paths to prison started with being commercially sexually exploited. In recently years, their stories have shed a light on this pervasive injustice.

Keiana's story is a devastating example of these systematic failures. She was sexually assaulted as a child, escaped her abusive home, and was sexually exploited as a homeless teenager on the streets of Sacramento. She cycled in and out of juvenile hall, but her needs as a victim of sexual abuse went unmet. After being caught up in a sting operation, she cooperated with authorities and testified against her trafficker. Despite her interaction with the court system as a cooperating victim witness, she was thrust back into life on the streets, and continued to be exploited. Relying on another minor for sustenance, she participated in the robbery of a grown man who was planning to buy her for commercial sex and the creation of pornography. She was arrested, charged as an adult despite being barely seventeen years old, convicted of multiple felonies, and sentenced to ten years in prison. She spent her eighteenth birthday through her twenty-fifth birthday behind bars, while the trauma she suffered as a teenage sex-trafficking victim remained untreated. There was no support system for her at critical junctures in her young life.

It is clear that young women ensnared in the sex trade need opportunities and ways to seek a fresh start. We must "begin at the beginning"—through education, support, and opportunity for kids who are at risk before they fall victim to trafficking. Frederick Douglass has been cited as saying, "It is easier to build strong children than to repair broken men." This was the foundational concept in Ashlie Bryant's work to build a human-trafficking-prevention education program. She partnered with an Atlanta-based nonprofit, the Frederick Douglass Initiative, founded by Ken Morris Jr., a descendent of both Frederick Douglass and Booker T. Washington, and Love Never Fails, an Oakland-based survivor-advocacy nonprofit focused on education.[6] Together, they are working to fulfill their mission to advance freedom and prevent human trafficking, through comprehensive education in classrooms across the country.

When prevention fails and kids are caught up in the criminal justice system with cases of their own, we need to look at them through a public-health lens: they are children who have been subjected to severe forms of sexual abuse and trauma. While, depending on the circumstances, they may need to be held accountable for voluntary criminal behavior, they also need medical and mental-health treatment for the trauma they have endured. Addressing criminal behavior without addressing the trauma that caused it is short-sighted, ineffective, and unfair. Commercially sexually exploited children should not be prosecuted as adults or sentenced to lengthy prison terms.

In addition to trauma-informed mental health treatment, access to reproductive health care is imperative. Traffickers frequently withhold birth control from victims as a way to track and control them. In other cases, victims are forced to terminate pregnancies or forced to carry pregnancies to term. These are deeply personal decisions that no one should be deprived of making for themselves. By taking this basic form of autonomy away from victims, sex traffickers further dehumanize them. Free access to a trusted health care provider is essential.

On the other side of the equation, we also need to address what is driving demand. Why do some men think it is okay to pay teenagers for sex acts? Is it entitlement—the idea that you can get whatever you want with money? Is it rape culture—a prevailing social attitude that has normalized or trivialized sexual abuse? Is it a lack of understanding or appreciation for the pain they are inflicting? Human-trafficking education in the classroom includes all students—not just would-be victims but would-be predators. Perhaps some will be deterred by hearing about the devastating consequences of human trafficking. But we need to continue fighting for a cultural shift to dismantle the stubborn legacy of misogyny and be a society that truly values women and girls.

Sex trafficking is on the extreme end of a continuum that includes sexual harassment and sexual abuse. It is also inextricably linked to the spectrum of pay inequity and labor exploitation. Many workers face wage theft, unfair working conditions, unsafe working conditions, threats, and sexual harassment from their bosses. Because of financial pressures and power dynamics, they may not feel they are able to report abuse, quit their jobs, or escape. In some cases, labor violations are extreme enough to constitute human trafficking, if workers are not free to leave. This is why training and awareness across multiple industries and government departments are so important.

Finally, the role of internet providers and social media companies in either stopping or proliferating online sexual abuse cannot be overstated. Social media platforms must be proactive in preventing human trafficking and the spread of child sexual exploitation through images on their sites. Technology always moves faster than the government or legal system leaving regulation of the internet incredibly challenging. The SESTA/FOSTA amendment to the CDA, which exempted sex trafficking from the law's otherwise-broad immunity, did not address other forms of abuse, crime, or disinformation perpetrated through the internet. Platforms may not see a financial incentive to act responsibly on their own, since abusive posts can be eye-catching and click-generating.[7]

Despite the exception for sex trafficking, the Communications Decency Act still provides broad cover to internet platforms that enable and proliferate harmful and criminal activity. Yet there is nothing stopping internet platforms from implementing moderation practices and quickly removing content that does not adhere to their user service agreements. Social media companies and internet services providers must take responsibility in curbing the harms caused by their products, especially when the lives of children are at stake.

Many companies do exercise corporate responsibility. Apple refused to develop an app for Backpage, for example. Chase refused to process payments when it knew the payments went to Backpage and were linked to sex trafficking. After brave survivors shared their stories, Mastercard, Discover, and Visa stopped processing payments to Pornhub, forcing the site to remove millions of videos depicting children being sexually assaulted.[8] Companies donate profits, hire survivors, and voluntarily educate employees to promote further awareness. But as a society we have fallen short and failed far too many children who have been victimized on Backpage and other websites.

Law enforcement can also work with technology companies to detect online warning signs and intervene before sexual abuse videos go viral or children are sold for commercial sex. Traffickers often use social media to identify, "friend" and groom vulnerable teenagers. Social media companies can partner with law enforcement to identify and intervene when appropriate as well as use hash data to quickly detect online images of sexual abuse and exploitation. This type of partnership is a critical tool in combating trafficking, both to protect children and apprehend predators. Thorn, the nonprofit we worked with on our very first Backpage operation, continues to work with law enforcement on tools to identify and prevent further online sexual exploitation of children. The National Center for Missing & Exploited Children has advanced innovative technology to help identify and rescue missing kids, using multiple strategies and serving as the national clearinghouse.

There is an inherent and complex tension among privacy interests, open-web interests, and the role of technology companies in moderating content and providing information to law enforcement. We need to protect a free exchange of ideas on the internet and the privacy of users, but this cannot be done in a vacuum without regard to our collective vulnerabilities or the unique vulnerabilities of children. First Amendment jurisprudence limits the definition of speech to exclude harmful and dangerous expression such as death threats and images depicting sexually assaulted children. Even speech that is considered protected can be subjected to reasonable time, place, and manner restrictions. But the broad interpretation of the CDA by some courts has extended the immunity afforded to online platforms well beyond the bounds of the First Amendment's protection. Congress should continue to explore balanced regulations to enhance internet safety and protect people from being abused. Ultimately, though, and regardless of the broad immunity that's been construed under the current CDA, social media companies should be vigilant in ensuring that their products do not facilitate online sex trafficking or any form of online abuse, especially the sexual abuse of children. Social media companies should also be at the table as we continue to strive for forward-thinking solutions to protect children and stop the unintended consequences of the booming tech industry.

Language matters, yet current law and common vernacular perpetuate words and phrases that continue to harm survivors and hold us back. Using the word "john," for example, to refer to an adult man who is buying sex acts with a sexually exploited teenager normalizes someone who is engaged in predatory and exploitive behavior. Even the terms pimp and pimping, which I have admittedly had difficulty avoiding throughout this book because they are enshrined in the California Penal Code, can be problematic, invoking harmful gendered and racialized imagery that distracts us from the realities of commercial sexual exploitation. Using the word "prostitute" or, worse, "child prostitute" defines people by their circumstances and wrongfully blames a victim for his or her own exploitation. A child who is being commercially sexually exploited is a rape victim. There's no such thing as a child prostitute.[9] A survivor who becomes a victim advocate and lends her expertise should be referred to as an "expert" or a "lived-experience expert." No one should be defined or limited by what they have endured, and it is important to empower survivors to define themselves and participate in anti-human-trafficking work on their own terms.

Once I attended a fundraiser supporting services for human-trafficking survivors with a young woman whom I had been mentoring. She was being honored at the event and was excited to be there with her daughter, showing off a new gold-and-white dress that looked absolutely stunning. We sat down at a fancily decorated table in a five-hundred-person ballroom and started making predictions about what the food would be. Then we noticed a menu-style agenda with the young woman's name and there in bold print, "Sex Trafficking Victim." "I didn't know they were going to say that about me," she said, stunned and humiliated. She was an accomplished working mom, finding time to advocate for her community, and yet in a room full of people who wanted to help, she was being exploited. "Sex-trafficking victim" was not a title she ever wanted. She had been tokenized. She deserved to be recognized and appreciated as more than the sum of her trauma.

Our approach to human trafficking must be inclusive, broad, and multifaceted. Teachers, counselors, police officers, and health care providers are all on the front lines and must be engaged and trained in ways that empower young people. Law enforcement should target those who exploit victims and should continue to build trust, particularly in vulnerable communities. This trust is relationship based and built through multidisciplinary task forces with community collaboration and survivor partnership. Government and the private and nonprofit sectors should work together to create opportunities for at-risk youth and sex-trafficking survivors, particularly girls and women of color who have been disproportionately impacted.

At the heart of all our work should be the survivors whom I have had the privilege to work with both in prosecuting Backpage and telling this story. They are incredible young women. It has been the honor of my life to stand with them as they speak up for justice. As we search for solutions to the global scourge of human trafficking, we must always listen to their voices and follow their lead.

ACKNOWLEDGMENTS

THIS book is dedicated to human-trafficking survivors who have had the courage to escape, to come forward, and to share their experiences. The anti-human-trafficking movement has been powered by survivors who have made deep sacrifices to insist on dignity and justice for all. I want to particularly acknowledge the work of Carissa Phelps, Leah Albright Byrd, Janette Diaz, Russell Wilson, Sara Kruzan, James Dold, Minh Dang, Holly Austin Smith, Sharan Dhanoa, Ashlie Bryant, Yiota Souras, Stefanie Richard, Nancy O'Malley, Rachelle and Loren Ditmore, Nilda Valmores, Sarai Smith-Mazariegos, Terri Galvan, Peggy Fava, Maheen Kaleem, Yasmin Vafa, and Vanessa Russell for their leadership in combating human trafficking and helping me to better understand it.

I also want to thank my compatriots at the Attorney General's Office who continue to inspire me with their exceptional work. There are too many to name, but here are a few: Randy Mailman, Jackie Salvi, Brian Fichtner, Reye Diaz, Darrell Early, Peter Williams, Jessica Owen, Amanda Plisner, Brett Morris, Suzi Gorsuch, and Scott Bachmann. I also want to thank Steve Oetting, Jim Root, Robert Morgester, and Jerry Engler for setting high expectations at DOJ and always leading by example. Thanks to Bethany Lesser and the press team for finding the right ways to talk about human trafficking and to Patricia Moscoso for encouraging me in writing this book. Thank you to former attorneys general Kamala Harris and Xavier Becerra for having the courage to take on this fight.

I also want to thank Kevin Rapp for his dedication and excellent work on the federal case and Bassam Banafa for his continued ingenuity and research.

I will always be grateful for the mentorship and inspiration I received from the late Dave Druliner—one of the best prosecutors who ever lived.

Thanks to my editor, Clara Platter, and the team at NYU Press for making this book better on every page, to publicist Angela Baggetta, and to my agent, Victoria Skurnick, for taking a chance on me.

Lastly, I want to thank my friends and family for your love and support and for always being on my side. I am grateful to my parents, who instilled in me a strong sense of justice and encouraged me in writing this book. And to my husband Cary and my sons, Ben and Tyler—you're my everything.

ACKNOWLEDGMENTS

NOTES

AUTHOR'S NOTE

1. Polaris, "Myths Facts and Statistics," accessed February 2020, www. polarisproject.org.
2. National Center for Missing & Exploited Children, "Data," accessed February 2020, www.missingkids.org; Cara Kelly, "13 Sex Trafficking Statistics That Explain the Enormity of the Global Sex Trade," *USA Today*, July 29, 2019, www.usatoday.com; US State Department, "Trafficking in Persons Report," June, 2019, www.state.gov.
3. Dan Whitcomb, "Exclusive: Report Gives Glimpse into Murky World of U.S. Prostitution in Post-Backpage Era," Reuters, April 11, 2019.

CHAPTER 1. THE MOTEL

1. Danna Basson, Jodie Langs, Kirsten Acker, Stacey Katz, Neha Desai, and Julian Ford, *Psychotherapy for Commercially Sexually Exploited Children: A Guide for Community-Based Behavioral Health Practitioners and Agencies* (Oakland, CA: WestCoast Children's Clinic, 2018), www.west-coastcc.org.
2. Holly Austin Smith, *Walking Prey: How America's Youth Are Vulnerable to Sex Slavery* (New York: St. Martin's, 2014), 35–36.
3. Todd Bookman, "Human Trafficking Survivor Settles Lawsuit against Motel Where She Was Held Captive," *All Things Considered*, NPR, February 20, 2020. Targeting motels for enabling sex trafficking has since been a successful legal tactic in both criminal and civil cases. See also Meghan Poole, "Beyond Hospitality: Hotel Liability for Human Trafficking," *Trafficking Matters*, Human Trafficking Institute, January 24, 2019, www. traffickingmatters.com.

CHAPTER 2. OPERATION WILTED FLOWER

1. Assembly Bill No. 22, Chapter 240, CA Penal Code (2006), www.leginfo. ca.gov.
2. Center for Public Policy Studies, "California Human Trafficking Fact Sheet," February 2013, www.centerforpublicpolicy.org.
3. CA Penal Code, § 266h.
4. Trafficking Victims Protection Act of 2000; see National Human Trafficking Hotline, "Federal Law," accessed May, 10, 2020, https:// humantraffickinghotline.org; and US Department of Justice, "Key Legislation," accessed May 10, 2020, www.justice.gov. Andrea Crossan, "How a Sweatshop Raid in an LA Suburb Changed the American Garment Industry," The World, December 5, 2017. pri.org.

5. Kamala D. Harris, *The State of Human Trafficking in California* (Sacramento: California Department of Justice, 2012), www.oag.ca.gov.

6. In the initial operation, we worked with My Sister's House, a trusted resource doing wonderful work for survivors in the Sacramento area: www.my-sisters-house.org.

7. People v. Bai Sacramento, case no. 13F02998 (California Superior Court, June, 14, 2013).

8. People v. Kwang, Lee, et al., case no. 601628A-D (Alameda County Superior Court, December 14, 2014); "Four Suspects Arrested for Alleged Sex Trafficking Ring," ABC 7 News, December 13, 2014, www.abc7news.com.

9. Jasmine Garsd, "Should Sex Work Be Decriminalized? Some Activists Say It's Time," *All Things Considered*, NPR, March 22, 2019, www.npr.org.

10. Holly Austin Smith, *Walking Prey: How America's Youth Are Vulnerable to Sex Slavery* (New York: St. Martin's, 2014).

CHAPTER 3. AMERICAN SEX TRAFFICKING

1. People v. Andrew Jordan, case no. NA102583 (Los Angeles County Superior Court, February 17, 2016).

2. Nicholas Kristof, "Every Parent's Nightmare," *New York Times*, March 10, 2016.

3. Grantmakers for Girls of Color, "Sex Trafficking's True Victims: Why Are Our Black Girls/Women So Vulnerable?" accessed January 18, 2021. https://www.grantmakersforgirlsofcolor.org.

4. CA Evidence Code, § 1161(b).

5. National Center on Domestic Violence, "Power and Control Wheel," accessed February 2020, www.ncdsv.org; World Health Organization, "Understanding and Addressing Violence against Women: Intimate Partner Violence," 2012, https://apps.who.int.

CHAPTER 4. BACKPAGE

1. Thorn, "About Us," accessed May 2020, www.thorn.org.

CHAPTER 5. THE BUSINESS

1. Declaration in Support of Arrest Warrant, People v. Ferrer et al., case no. 16FE019224 (Sacramento County Superior Court, September 29, 2016).

2. Lisa Gray, "An Editor on the Lam: And a $5K Check out of the Blue," *Houston Chronicle*, October 8, 2016.

3. Matthew Hendley, "Joe Arpaio Loses: New Times Co-founders Win $3.75 Million Settlement for 2007 False Arrests," *Phoenix New Times*, December 30, 2013, www.phoenixnewtimes.com.

4. Michael Keifer, "Phoenix New Times Founders Selling Company," *Arizona Republic*, September 23, 2012, www.archive.azcentral.com.

5. CA Penal Code § 1546.

6. Declaration in Support of Arrest Warrant, People v. Ferrer et al.

7. Brady v. Maryland, 373 U.S. 83 (1963).

CHAPTER 7. FLIGHT 21

1. CA Penal Code § 1548–58; Uniform Criminal Extradition Act, 18 U.S.C. § 3182.

CHAPTER 8. ROUND 1

1. People's Supplemental Brief in Opposition to Defendants' Demurrer to Felony Complaint, People v. Ferrer et al., case no. 16FE019224 (Sacramento County Superior Court, November 28, 2016).
2. People's Supplemental Brief.
3. People v. Ferrer et al., case no. 16FE019224 (Sacramento County Superior Court, December 9, 2016, Ruling of Judge Bowman).
4. US Senators Rob Portman and Claire McCaskill, United States Senate Permanent Subcommittee on Investigations, *Backpage.com's Knowing Facilitation of Sex Trafficking* (Washington, DC: US Government Publishing Office, 2017), www.hsgac.senate.gov.

CHAPTER 9. WINTER

1. Tom Jackman and Jonathan O'Connell, "16-Year-Old Was Found Beaten, Stabbed to Death after Being Advertised as a Prostitute on Backpage," *Washington Post*, July 11, 2017, www.washingtonpost.com.
2. US Senators Rob Portman and Claire McCaskill, United States Senate Permanent Subcommittee on Investigations, *Backpage.com's Knowing Facilitation of Sex Trafficking* (Washington, DC: US Government Publishing Office, 2017), www.hsgac.senate.gov.
3. Backpage was eventually sanctioned for misleading the court in other civil cases. "For the reasons set forth above, the Court concludes that during this litigation, Backpage knowingly and repeatedly made false representations of fact concerning relevant aspects of its operations. This fraudulent conduct has been pervasive throughout this law suit." Backpage v. Dart, case no. 1:15-cv-06340 (US District Court for the Northern District of Illinois, March 25, 2018, Ruling of Judge John J. Tharp); see also Alexis Krell, "Backpage.com Sanctioned by Pierce County Judge in Lawsuit after CEO's Guilty Plea," *Tacoma (WA) News Tribune*, July 2, 2018, www.thenewstribune.com.
4. Transcript of oral argument, People v. Ferrer et al., case no. 16FE024013 (Sacramento Superior Court, July 17, 2017).
5. Transcript of oral argument.
6. See 3Strands Global Foundation, "Join the Movement," accessed May 2020, www.3strandsglobalfoundation.org.
7. People v. Ferrer et al., case no. 16FE024013 (Sacramento Superior Court, August 23, 2017).

CHAPTER 10. THE BREAKDOWN

1. People v. Bollaert, 248 Cal. App. 4th 699 (2016).
2. Laura J. Lederer and Christopher A. Wetzel, "The Health Consequences of Sex Trafficking and Their Implications for Identifying Victims in Healthcare Facilities," *Annals of Health and Law* 23, no. 1 (2014), www.globalcenturion.org.

3. Superseding Indictment, United States of America v. Lacey et al., case no. 2:18-cr-00422-SPL (US District Court for the District of Arizona, 2018).

AFTERWORD

1. Dan Whitcomb, "Exclusive: Report Gives Glimpse into Murky World of U.S. Prostitution in Post-Backpage Era," Reuters, April 11, 2019, www.reuters.com.

2. Carissa Phelps, *Run Away Girl: Escaping Life on the Streets* (New York: Viking, 2012).

3. Malika Saada Saar, Rebecca Epstein, Lindsay Rosenthal, and Yasmin Vafa, *The Sexual Abuse to Prison Pipeline: The Girls' Story* (Washington, DC: Center on Poverty and Inequality, Georgetown Law, 2015), www.rights-4girls.org.

4. Maggy Krell and Maheen Kaleem, "How California Is Failing Vulnerable Victims of Systemic Racism," Washington Post, October 28, 2020, https://www.washingtonpost.com.

5. Bobby Allyn, "Cyntoia Brown Released after 15 Years in Prison for Murder," NPR, August 7, 2019, www.npr.org.

6. Fredrick Douglass Family Initiatives, "Kenneth B. Morris, Jr.," accessed May 2020, www.fdfi.org; Love Never Fails, accessed May 2020, www.lovenever-failsus.com.

7. Danielle Keats Citron and Mary Anne Franks, "The Internet as a Speech Machine and Other Myths Confounding Section 230 Reform" (Public Law Research Paper No. 20-8, Boston University School of Law, February 2020).

8. Nicholas Kristof, "An Uplifting Update, on the Terrible World of Pornhub", New York Times, December 9, 2020, nytimes.com; Jordan Valinsky, "Pornhub Removes a Majority of Its Videos after Investigation Reveals Child Abuse," CNN Business, December 15, 2020, cnn.com.

9. T. Ortiz Walker Pettigrew, rights4girls, https://rights4girls.org/campaign/, accessed December 19, 2020.

ABOUT THE AUTHOR

MAGGY KRELL is a legal trailblazer who has taken on high-impact cases as both a criminal prosecutor and civil practitioner. She has fought for reproductive justice and access to health care as Chief Legal Counsel for Planned Parenthood Affiliates of California and also successfully represented migrant families who were forcefully separated and detained during President Trump's family separation policy. She was a criminal prosecutor for fifteen years, serving as Supervising Deputy Attorney General of the Special Crimes Unit, and cross-designated as a Special Assistant United States Attorney. She prosecuted high-profile cases throughout California, including murder, organized crime, human trafficking, domestic violence, white-collar crime, and mortgage fraud. Her most notable accomplishments stem from her tireless efforts to combat human trafficking and protect and empower crime victims, including her groundbreaking prosecution of the sex-trafficking website Backpage.com.